The Greatest Guide to Sex

This is a **GREATEST**GUIDES title

Greatest Guides Limited, Woodstock, Bridge End, Warwick CV34 6PD, United Kingdom

www.greatestguides.com

Series created by Harshad Kotecha

Greatest Guides is committed to a sustainable future for our planet. This book is printed on paper certified by the Forest Stewardship Council.

Printed and bound in the United Kingdom

ISBN 978-1-907906-02-2

To my wonderful husband
Patrick Pearson.

Thank you so much for your vision, your wit,
and your inspired way with words.

This book would not have been written without
your love, support, faith, patience, sense of fun –
and collaboration (in every way!)

Contents

Foreword

Julie's easy way with words flows through this compelling sex guide like fine wine. With a wicked sense of humor she educates on all matters sexual and continually surprises the reader with fascinating sex trivia. Do you know that Dr John Harvey Kellogg invented his cornflakes as a libido suppressant, or that it was commonplace at the end of the 19th Century for doctors to masturbate female patients to orgasm to treat sexual desire, known then as 'hysteria'? Julie does.

This guide is perfect bedside reading for couples, addressing men's needs as well as women's, with lessons for him in how to exercise his pelvic floor muscles for sexual benefits. Yes, men have them too. And tricky topics are thoroughly tackled from faked orgasms to having sex during periods to vagina size issues. In between you'll find every tip you need to improve your sex life and boost your orgasmic potential from 'good' to 'oh my God!'.

An air of confident authority prevails throughout, but reading The Greatest Guide to Sex still feels as comfortable as having a chat with an old friend down at the local pub. If only all friends were so well-informed...

Sarah Hedley, author of *7 Days to Amazing Sex*

“ There are many people who have questions about sex and this book provides some honest and often fascinating answers. Julie has written an informative, frank and humorous guide which gives great tips for improving your sex life. Packed with techniques you may have tried and others you'd never dreamed of, this is a really enjoyable read for anyone looking to spice up their love life or simply find out more about sex. ”

Dr Catherine Hood
Sexual health & relationships expert

“ Quirky, clever and packed with enough tantalising facts and stats to make you the star of a hundred dinner parties. ”

Tracey Cox
Sex & relationships expert and best-selling author

“ Use this book! I very rarely meet people who are totally satisfied with their love life, yet most of us guys make little effort to improve things. Here's a great, easy way to get things going in the right direction – once a week stay in bed with your lover and try one new tip from this book. Before you know it you will have re-energized your love making! ”

Mimo Antonucci
Founder of www.sensualessentials.com

“ Anyone who knows Julie knows that she is one incredibly sexy woman and now we know why! Scandalous, delightful, this book is a must read for anyone who prefers being awake during sex and smiling after it. I was supposed to be getting ready for an afternoon of work but after reading this book I think I'm off to play... ”

Jenni Trent Hughes
Relationship counsellor

A few words from Julie…

I've always refused to believe that our sex lives have to become boring, or even completely disintegrate, as we settle down in a relationship. Don't get me wrong – I do acknowledge that the steamy euphoria of the initial six months has to calm down, so you can put your knickers back on and pay the bills. I just don't accept sinking into the inevitability of cosy slippers and cups of tea, when we may also yearn for a spark of passion to relight our fire.

This book has been written for anyone who wants to put some fun into their lovemaking and broaden their sexual horizons – regardless of age, sexual orientation, whether you've been in a relationship for years or are newly enjoying each other. I have sought out tips that I hope will inform, inspire and ultimately improve what is such an important aspect of our lives – and they're all tried and tested.

Sex is universal – we wouldn't be here without it – and there's always room for improvement. We're very focussed today on personal development – we're constantly being urged to move out of our comfort zones and to set goals for our careers, fitness levels, finances, weight-loss … why don't we have some fun and set a few for our sex lives too?

I hope you find this guide amusing, enlightening, reassuring, and of course stimulating – and I also hope you have as much fun reading it as I've had putting it all together!

With love,

Julie x

Chapter 1

Kiss and Make out

The first sexually intimate act most of us experience is a kiss. Whether it's behind the school bike-sheds, in a darkened shop doorway or, like mine, in the seductive environment of our local fish finger factory, that heady excitement of another's lips pressed against yours is wonderful...if you're lucky.

In *Gone with the Wind* Clark Gable declares to Vivien Leigh "You should be kissed, and often, and by someone who knows how". Yes please, Rhett. There are many talented kissers in the world who've elevated this simple act into an art form, but sadly there are others whose technique leaves a lot to be desired.

If you think you've been neglecting your snogging skills – or you know someone who has – it's worth polishing them up. The lips are a major erogenous zone, in fact practitioners of tantric sex advocate a gentle sucking of the lips, crediting them with a hotline to the genitals.

Research by the Marriage Guidance Council indicates that when a relationship deteriorates, kissing is one of the first things to go – but if you make an effort to put it back on the menu, it can rekindle the romance and emotional bond between you.

Even if you're completely satisfied with your partner, you may still be longing for more opportunities to pucker up – a top psychotherapist recently revealed that the number of times an average couple kiss is four-and-a-half pecks a day. That's Good Morning, Hello, Goodbye and Goodnight (which presumably lasts a bit longer and accounts for the half). Read on for some lip-smacking how's, why's, do's and don'ts.

Kiss me, honey honey...

Try planting tiny delicate kisses all over your loved one's face to gently wake them up in the morning. The secret is to make the touch of your lips as soft and tender as possible – be as light as a feather, especially around the eyes and eyelids. Take your time – this isn't one to attempt with the clock ticking, but it makes for an intimate and magical start to the day.

Upside down canoodle

I know this might sound a little strange, but it's good for a giggle if nothing else. (Hell, if Kirsten Dunst can enjoy it with Spiderman, who are we to criticize?) Best performed on the bed or floor, one partner's lips are upside down to the other partner's, so your mouths are top lip to bottom lip. Added bonus: if the person on top crawls forward you're in a perfect 69 position – could be handy.

10 reasons to banish the stiff upper lip

1. Ann Summers has compiled a survey of the sexiest turn-ons, and a good old-fashioned kiss comes in at Number One.

2. Dentists suggest that it's good for the teeth. Kissing can help prevent plaque build-up, because the saliva we produce neutralizes the natural acids in the mouth.

3. A kiss is quite a complex operation, requiring over 30 muscles working in harmony, and burning around 100 calories an hour.

4. Passionate kisses release the 'bonding' hormone oxytocin which is associated with fidelity, so lots of lip action means you're less likely to stray.

5. The UK has a National Kissing Day on July 6th, so that's a tailor-made excuse to grab Debbie from Accounts and show her your credentials.

6. Kissing improves your immunity. There are around 400 different micro-organisms in the average mouth – about 80% of these are common to everyone, whilst 20% are uniquely yours. When we lock lips and swap saliva, our immune system creates antibodies to deal with any foreign bacteria. This process is called 'cross-immunotherapy' and it helps us to fight infection.

7. A recent study suggests that people who give their partner a goodbye kiss before going to work have 20-30% higher incomes than those who don't! Psychologists believe the morning kiss generates a more positive outlook on the day ahead.

8. Kissing helps to tone the muscles in your cheeks and jaw, so they are less likely to sag.

9. Serial kissers suffer less with hay fever. Japanese researchers have found that half an hour of kissing can prevent our immune systems from producing histamine, the chemical responsible for runny noses and itchy eyes.

10. A steamy session of Philematology (the science of kissing) boosts self-esteem and relieves stress. And hiccups.

The eyes have it...

In her book *Things a Woman Should Know About Seduction* Emily Dubberley offers some intriguing advice. "By far the most powerful seductress's trick is the eye-to-lip glance. First, make eye contact. Leisurely drop your gaze to your object of your desire's lips, then return to his eyes. Repeat this. By the third time you look at his lips, he'll be drawn to kiss you. This one has an unnervingly high rate of success."

Staying power

The world's longest recorded smacker took place in New York in 2005 and lasted 30 hours, 59 minutes and 27 seconds. (Now that's what I call a kiss.)

Merci please

If the idea of French kissing, for either you or your partner, seems as distant as St. Tropez, experiment with kissing concentrating only on the lips – no tongues allowed. Take lots of time to lick, nibble, suck and truly relish the sensation. Not only will it send waves of pleasure coursing through to your nether regions, but it's a clever way of making you crave deeper, more intimate kissing again – as in 'abstinence makes the tongue grow fonder'.

12 Lip-action Do's and Don'ts

Do...clean your teeth – and your tongue whilst you're at it (pink and smooth wins over white and furry) and don't forget to floss to ensure a super-sweet mouth. If your lips have a tendency to get chapped, moisturize them with lip balm.

Do...vary the tempo. Start slow and sensual, then get more urgent and intense as your passion builds – it's much more exciting to be a bit unpredictable.

Do...gently hold and caress your partner's head or face as you're locking lips.

Do...tell each other, and demonstrate, how you like to be kissed – feedback is vital in order to really get it right. And watch each other's reactions too – if your loved one is blissed out, motionless and their eyes are still closed when you pull back, you can safely assume you got it right.

Do...grab every chance to enjoy a quick clinch – and make it a habit you keep up.

Do...make it last. Long, heady, toe-curling French kisses are good for the soul – possibly why they're sometimes known as 'soul kisses'.

Don't...dive straight in and start playing tonsil hockey. Invite your lover in gently by parting your lips a little. Then trace the tip of your tongue around their lips – and explore a little further before you finally intertwine tongues.

Don't...just think of kissing as a prelude to other things – it's valuable in its own right.

Don't...smoke. Try to give up if you possibly can – for every health reason going. Ashtray breath also rates high on the kissing turn-offs list.

Don't...slobber over your partner. Swallow any saliva that's surplus to requirements.

Don't...even go there if you have a cold sore. Caused by the herpes simplex virus, cold sores are highly contagious and passed on through infected saliva, so steer clear of smooching until they're past tense.

Don't...forget to look deep into each other's eyes between kisses – and never underestimate the importance of the Kiss.

The kiss of life

It's a harsh truth guys, but in the snogging stakes you're falling short of the mark. Apparently 95% of young women are not satisfied with their quota when it comes to puckering up – and the older ones aren't grinning from ear to ear either. Basically, kissing is to most women what blow jobs are to men – it's one of the things we love most, but don't usually get enough of. Become a champion at delivering great lip service and you've just about got it made. What's more, many women also believe that men who can't or don't kiss are rubbish in bed, so please double our doses – or you might never find out just how good it makes us feel...

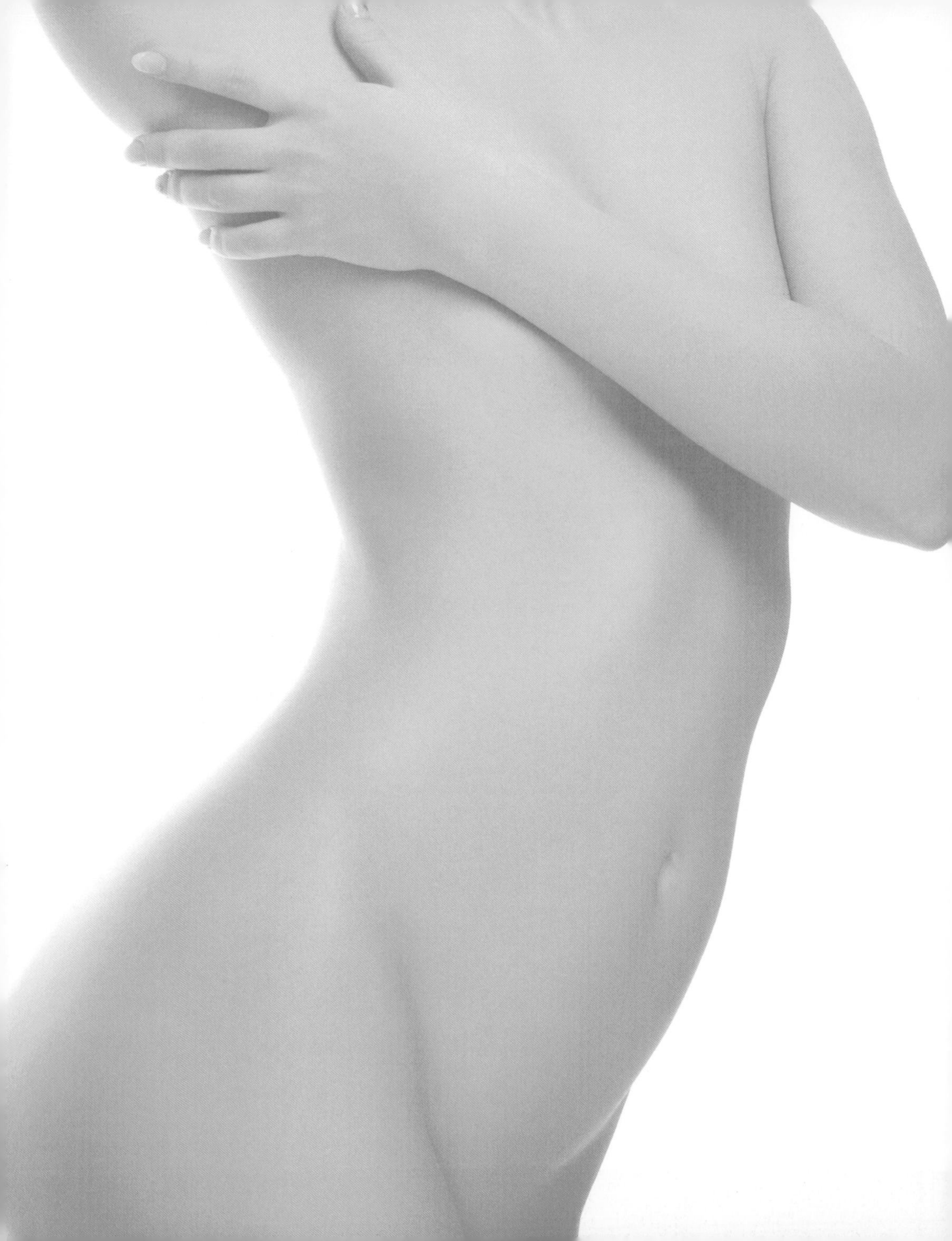

Chapter 2

A Grand Opening

The ancient Indian sex manual, The *Kama Sutra*, identifies three types of vagina. According to size, women are either a deer, a mare or – wait for it – an elephant. I know there's a charming British expression that if a woman is rather roomy down below, making love to her is like 'chucking a sausage down Oxford Street'. Seems they weren't averse to the odd insult back in 4th Century India, either.

Vaginas are created in all shapes, sizes and colors. The average human vagina is about 4 inches (10cm) long, and is a muscular tube that expands or contracts to accommodate a finger, penis, or a baby.

The term 'vagina' is often used to describe the female genitalia but is, in fact, only the passageway connecting the external bits to the uterus, with the cervix at its upper end. The proper name for our private parts is pudenda (not often used), vulva (most often used), or split beaver (only kidding).

Women can be shy about their vulvas – they're not normally on show, except to our lovers (and sometimes not even then if we're very self conscious). Inner labia are often a source of potential embarrassment – some are dark and wrinkly, some small and pale, some hang down, some have one lip longer than the other. Whatever your particular configuration, trust me – there are no genital deformities, only variations on a theme. Some tribeswomen in Africa even take pains (literally) to weight their labia down, to develop a desirable 7-inch dangle.

Whatever turns you on, I say – viva la vulva!

The magic button …

The clitoris has 8,000 nerve endings (twice as many as the penis) and is the most sensitive organ in the human body – in fact it's even more responsive than our tongues. Made up of eighteen parts, some visible, some hidden, it's also the only body part designed solely to give pleasure to its owner.

The bare essentials

Show off your booty with a Hollywood. Whether your preferred method is to wax (aagh!) or shave (get partner to do it?) the overall porn star effect is powerfully erotic. There's something so illicit about being completely exposed, and the total lack of hair makes your whole vulva even more sensitive. But if taking it all off is just too 'little girl-like', you could opt for a Brazilian, and leave a narrow landing strip above your bare labia. Alternatively try the American favorite, 'the Tiffany Box' – all pubes removed except for a tiny square, which is then dyed that famous shade of blue… Who's for Breakfast? (See Matching collar and cuffs, page 23)

A close shave

For an easy, pain-free path to pubic grooming, try a specialist shaving system such as the Smoothshave Intimate Area Shaver. It's a nifty little battery operated number that's designed specifically for use on stubble, promising to leave skin as smooth as a baby's bottom – in fact the only accompaniment needed is baby talc, making it feel surprisingly safe to use (Great for guys, too – see Supersize me, page 31.)

Little Miss Muff(et)

On the other hand, if you prefer not to prune your bush, then I have it on very good authority that some men find a couple of stray pubes poking out of your panties to be a massive turn-on. Just one or two little 'spider's legs' is apparently all it takes…

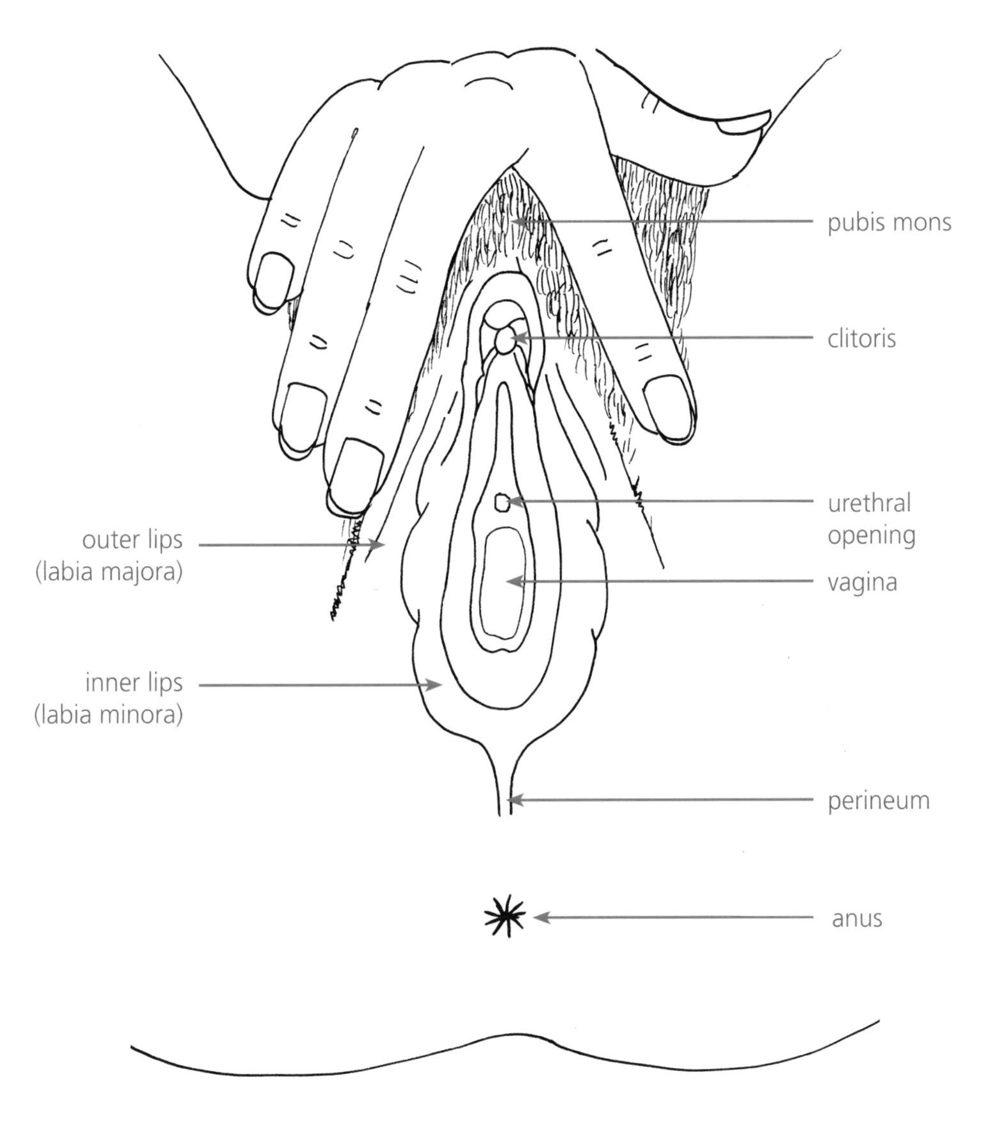

THE FEMALE GENITALIA

Taking the curse off things

Lots of women report feeling extra horny when they're having their period. This could be due to a number of reasons: see-sawing hormone levels can make you bolder sexually, nerve endings are at their most responsive at this time, and you may be less uptight about getting pregnant, if that's an issue (although this can still happen).

As an orgasm is also a great cure for period pains and cramps, there's no reason why you shouldn't make love, providing neither of you is put off or worried about any potential mess. Keep the wet wipes handy just in case, and maybe place a towel underneath you to save the sheets. Use some lube if you've just removed a tampon, and it's better to choose a position where he's on top – your blood flow is likely to be reduced when you're lying down. It also helps to pop a pillow under your bottom to raise your pelvis.

Ideally wait until the heaviest days are over, but if you want the freedom of having sex at any point in your cycle, then it might be worth trying the porn stars' secret weapon, Beppy Stringless Tampons or Sea Pearls (used if having to shoot scenes whilst menstruating). They are both sponges, and although they're not cheap, they are effective and easy to wear during lovemaking, plus they're discreet – so you can both just forget it's that time of the month.

Mirror, mirror on the wall…

When you have time and you know you won't be disturbed, sit down and get familiar with your personal geography. Take a look at your vulva with a hand-held mirror, and tell yourself that what you see is normal and natural. If you find you're experiencing negative feelings, don't suppress them – but don't dwell on them either. Many women think their ladybits are ugly or disfigured – let me reassure you that in 99.9% of cases they're not, and luckily any man, or same-sex partner, who wants to become intimately acquainted with your nether regions is biologically programmed to find the sight – and smell – extremely arousing.

There is a current trend for 'designer vaginas' where the labia are surgically 'tidied up' in a cosmetic procedure called labiaplasty, with a hefty price tag to match. But medical bodies claim that "it's a fashion being driven by commercial and media pressures that exploit women's insecurities, and is fraught with unknowns – including a risk to sexual arousal." If your body loathing in this area is so intense it's affecting your everyday life, do get the opinion of a reputable, qualified practitioner before considering anything – it's a high price to pay for a potentially dangerous procedure.

An easier, cheaper and immediately effective way to become more comfortable with how you look downstairs, is to check out the excellent photographs in *Femalia* by Joani Blank, or the frank and informative drawings in *Sex for One* by the great sexual pioneer, Betty Dodson. Both books are tasteful, non-sensational, and celebrate female sexuality in all its vulvic glory. You can also view photos and get a wealth of info from the Vulval Health Awareness Campaign website www.vhac.org

“ It is amazing how few women really know what their external anatomy looks like. Sadly, most girls are led to believe that they are 'dirty down there' and are therefore reluctant to examine themselves. Boys, however, are usually socialized to believe they possess a treasure in which to take a pride. ” Toni Weschler, fertility educator

Elusive but effusive

One theory about the G-spot is that it's actually the root of the clitoris. Another is that it protects the urethra during intercourse, which is why it's also called the urethral sponge. Since its discovery in the 1940s by the German gynecologist Ernst Grafenberg, the G-spot has spawned various theories and aroused heated debate. Most women today agree that it certainly arouses something – however, you need to find it first and that isn't always easy.

It's best to locate your G-spot when you've emptied your bladder and you're sitting down or squatting, but you can also lie on your stomach, or on your back – whichever suits you best. Place your palm face-down on your vulva, and insert a lubricated finger inside yourself, crooking it forward towards your pubic bone. You're looking for a swelling directly behind this bone, that's only an inch or so (2-4 cms) inside your vagina – much nearer the entrance than you might imagine. It's a pronounced, spongy lump, around the size of a bean, on the front wall (the side closest to your tummy) and it feels more ridged in texture than the surrounding vaginal walls. Don't confuse it with the cervix, which is a smooth protuberance sited much higher up.

If you're having trouble locating your G-spot, try getting your partner in on the act, or play around with a specially curved vibrator or dildo. It's also easier to find after you've had an orgasm, because it gets slightly harder and increases in size, becoming more like a walnut than a bean. And if you feel like you want to pee, it's because the G-spot shares a nerve with the bladder – this is a completely normal sensation, which will subside.

No matter how aroused they are, some women don't find the G-spot does anything for them, and some even dispute its existence. Others find it so intense that they go to heaven and back with a monumental climax, and a lucky few also ejaculate – or 'squirt' – varying amounts of fluid (which isn't urine) if they reach orgasm this way. To find out how, see Going with the flow, page 47 – and enjoy the search!

My plaice or yours?

Did you know that a man is actually partially responsible for his partner's smell down below? Sperm is highly alkaline and it causes the pH (acid/alkali) levels inside the vagina to rise, allowing unhealthy bacteria to take hold. Usually the body quickly restores the balance, especially when the sperm is familiar (as it is with a regular partner). But it's trickier to correct if a woman has unprotected sex with one or more new partners, and can often result in a strong 'fishy' smell.

Matching collar and cuffs

Hair dyes have now been developed for the nether regions (as regular hair dye is too strong). Minikini's safe, non-drip formula has been created for use around our most sensitive area, with a range of colors including sexy pink, brazen blue and golden blonde. It's great for guys too (OK, maybe not the pink) but it's effective for covering any unsightly gray pubes, and restoring his chest hair to its former Saturday Night Fever glory. The color doesn't rub off on underwear, and it won't run when you get hot and bothered either. Match the thatch to your natural hair color and feel safe in the process – with organic ingredients it's ammonia and parabens-free, and not tested on animals.

Now you really can get away with calling yourself a natural blonde…

Get a grip

Many years ago in Bangkok, I found myself in the privileged position of watching an accomplished Thai dancer shoot ping-pong balls from her vagina. She then progressed to smoking a cigar, using only the iron grip of her pelvic floor muscles. This is not easy. I know because I've tried. My horrified partner found me in our hotel room with one of his finest Havanas protruding from my pudenda – and things were never quite the same again.

Strong pelvic floor muscles are crucial for optimum sexual health. Otherwise known as PC or Kegel muscles, they support all the pelvic organs, and are the ones that contract during orgasm. Originally pioneered by Dr. Arnold Kegel in the 1940s (who discovered their sensual side-effects when he helped women overcome incontinence problems) they're the same muscles we use to stop ourselves peeing mid-flow. So not only will well-toned PCs give you greater bladder control, they'll also improve the frequency and force of your orgasms – and do wonders for keeping you tight down below (especially after childbirth).

The extra bonus is that you can discreetly squeeze and release, when and where you like – start with 25 clenches, twice a day, and build up to 50, holding each time for a count of two. If you're not good at remembering though, and only end up doing a random clench at the bus stop occasionally, there are several devices you can invest in for a proper workout, including the Kegel8 Tight & Tone which works electronically – with noticeable results in weeks.

Either way, consciously exercising your Kegels will enhance every aspect of your sex life, giving your man a vaginal embrace he's not likely to forget. You'll be playing ping-pong before you know it.

“The Vagina: aka bearded clam, boogina, choochi snorcher, smoo, fluffy sausage wallet, growler, mushy-mushy, hairy manilow, panty hamster, poonani, madge, tuna melt, tinkleflower.”

Chapter 3

A Handler's Guide

Penis size varies enormously, but the average range is between 2 to 4 inches at rest (5–10cm) and 5 to 7 inches (13–18cm) when standing to attention, with an erect circumference of 4½ inches (11½cm). I'm launching straight into measurements here, because numerous surveys suggest that men are just a tad preoccupied with the size of their members. It seems almost all of you – regardless of sexual orientation – wish you had a bigger one. (Stop looking for that tape measure.)

As Sarah Hedley writes in *Sex by Numbers*, "sex researcher Alfred Kinsey conducted a survey of the penis in the 1940s and concluded that the average length was 6 5⁄16 inches (16cm). However, it seems many of Kinsey's subjects were stretching the truth (and the measurements) adding an extra ½ inch (1cm) or so when they were left alone to mark down their length. Bless."

The irony is most women aren't too fussed, in fact 98% of us are turned on by our lover's penis, whatever its size. As the average length of the female vagina is just 4 inches (10cm) with only the first third being really sensitive, you don't have to be hung like a donkey to be a great lover – we quite like you at the shallow end sometimes. (Equally, if you are hung like a donkey and reading this, I'm sure you've given rides to some very appreciative admirers… I bet your toffee apples are a sight to behold, too.)

Like vulvas, penises come in all shapes, sizes and colors – and you know what? They're all works of art.

The hotspots

It's a good idea for women to familiarize themselves with the supersensitive bits of their man's member. Generally the head of the penis tends to be much more responsive than the base. Most supercharged of all are:

Glans – the head or 'helmet' – choc-full of nerve endings (many more than the shaft). Permanently on view if a man is circumcised, in uncircumcised men it can be seen when the penis is erect or with the foreskin rolled back.

Coronal rim – the tender rim of the glans. Also known as the crown (hence 'the Crown Jewels'?)

Frenulum – the ultra-sensitive strand of skin joining the head and shaft, on the underside of the penis. High-ranking erogenous zone.

Shaft – the main body of the penis, which fills up with blood and hardens during arousal.

Scrotum – the soft, wrinkly pouch which protects the testicles, as they work their socks off to produce around 300 million sperm a day. (Each ejaculation spills between 200 and 600 million of them.)

Perineum – the area between the balls and the anus – also a major erogenous zone.

Glisten up

We've all got used to the idea of men using moisturizers for a healthy facial glow – why not extend this to your penis? Women love a velvety smooth shaft, so preen your pole with a good body lotion or massage oil. It'll have the same beneficial effect and you'll have more fun applying it!

A word of warning – if you use baby oil, remove it before having intercourse. It's not good for a woman's vagina as it can cause a yeast infection, and it will also rot condoms.

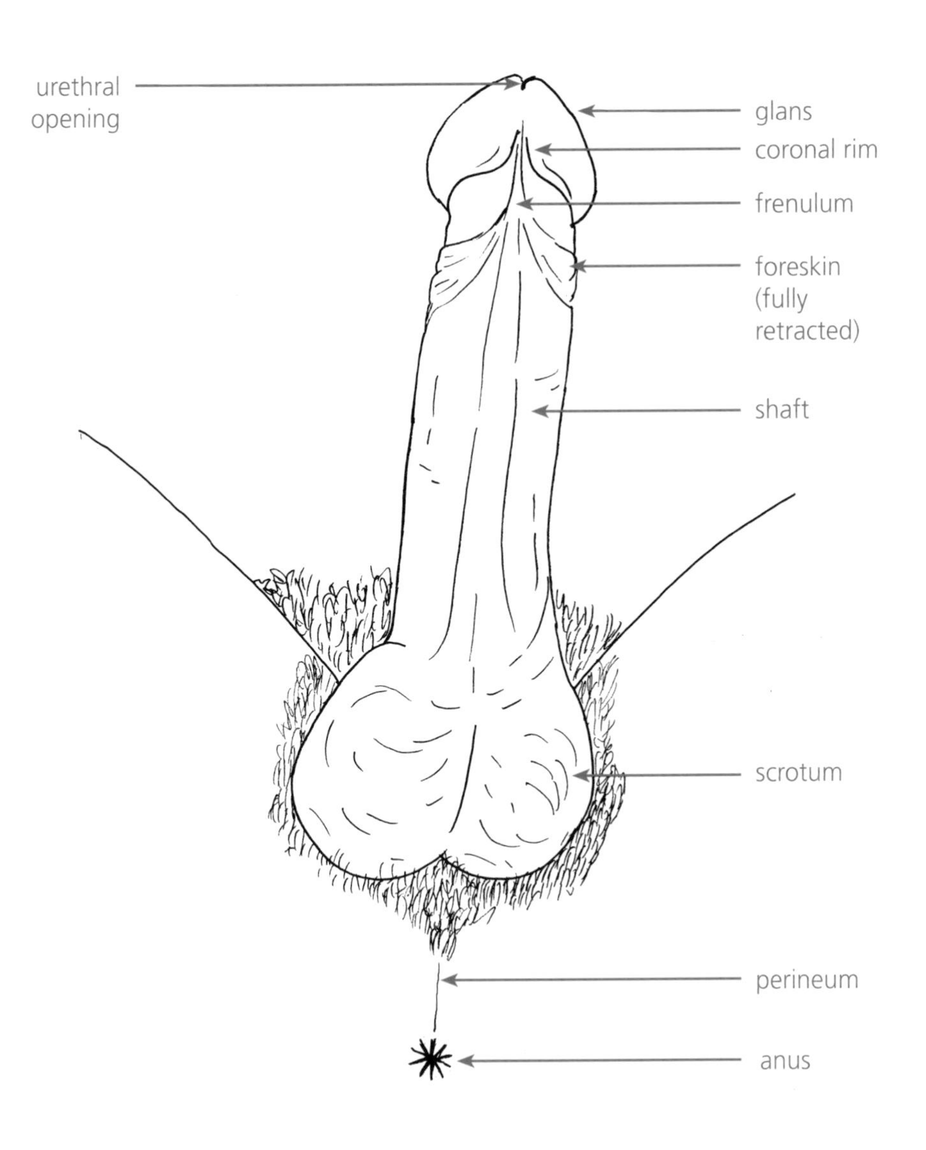

THE MALE GENITALIA

Measuring up

I have it on very good authority that blokes are never quite sure exactly how to measure their manhoods, so here's the correct method, according to American doctor, Harold Reed, MD:

- While standing, make your penis erect
- Angle your penis down until it is parallel to the floor
- Set a ruler against your pubic bone just above the base of your penis, and measure to the tip
- Now wash the ruler

Disposable dong

The human penis is huge in relation to the rest of the male anatomy and is, in fact, one of the largest organs amongst the world's primates. OK, so the blue whale has a weapon that can measure up to three and a half meters, with the African elephant coming in at two meters, but good old Homo Sapiens still manages to knock spots off the gorilla, with its meagre two inch offering (when erect). Only a barnacle has a bigger willy relative to its body size than Man, though it does enjoy the unique privilege of being able to throw it away every year and grow a new one.

Stress solution

Semen could have anti-depressant qualities (and no, that doesn't mean we want to swallow it three times a day). Tests have revealed that it contains a neurotransmitter called dopamine, which makes us feel happy, fulfilled – and all warm and fuzzy. It's also indicated that women who have condom-free sex with one regular partner, have lower levels of depression. (Oh, go on then big boy, bring it on...)

Seeds for seed

The amount of semen produced in an average ejaculation is one to two teaspoons, but the volume and potency vary according to the age and general health of the individual. Frequency of orgasm affects quantity too – you'll notice a difference if you hold back for a day or two, as opposed to bashing one out every few hours.

Stock up sperm supplies by increasing fluid intake and eating foods rich in zinc – essential for sperm formation, prostate health and the production of testosterone. Good sources include pumpkin seeds, shellfish, red meat, crab, eggs, wheatgerm and peanuts.

Willy nilly

To be the stiffest, most super-charged stud on the block, steer clear of excessive beer and cigarettes. A couple of smokes can quickly knock out a third of blood flow to the penis. And beer doesn't tick any boxes either, causing prostate difficulties as well as brewer's droop. A study in Hawaii of more than 6,500 men, revealed some prostate gland problems after – shock/horror – even just three bottles of beer a month! Beer stimulates secretion of the hormone prolactin, linked with a diminished sex drive and possible impotence – so go a little easy on the pints.

Supersize me

OK guys, listen up. If you're sporting a tangled Brillo pad between your legs, then some pubic grooming never goes amiss. And if you still believe that bigger is better (it's not necessarily) you can give yourselves instant length by cutting back the hair from around the base of your penis. The effect is surprisingly impressive, giving the illusion that you're a good inch longer. Trim very carefully with nail scissors, or use an intimate area shaver, which is great for backs, sacks and cracks. Go on, pinch an inch – who cares if it's all done with mirrors?

Free willy

Ditching your underpants (i.e. 'going commando' or 'freeballing') is becoming increasingly fashionable. Some men are doing it on a daily basis, others are swinging free semi-regularly, but it's gaining in popularity all the time. Biggest advantages are that it's better for your fertility as your testicles aren't restricted by anything (tight underwear decreases sperm count) and it could increase the sensitivity of your penis. Your partner may also find it sexy to discover your dangly bits let loose – with easy access for a quick fondle – in fact it rates as Number 36 on Ann Summers' compilation of the 100 sexiest turn-ons.

Sexual healing

Applying pressure to the upper part of a man's heel can produce rather pleasant sensations in their nether regions. But reflexology isn't just reserved for the feet or hands – try making tiny circular motions with two fingers to gently massage the back of his penis. Start at the base and work towards the tip, with your other hand cradling his testicles. 'Penis reflexology' is all about linking different parts of his shaft with sexual energy, and restoring normal working order if that's been lacking.

Rising to the occasion

There's a funny story about an actor, famous in the 70s, who was always cast as villains or 'hard men'. This might have had something to do with the fact that he was something of a hard man himself – in more ways than one. Not only was he known for his acting and his criminal exploits, but he developed a novel party piece, which he showed off to great acclaim in the pub. Being blessed with an absolutely enormous cock, and pelvic floor muscles of steel, he could reputedly hang four half-pint tankards on his proud and rigid member. Rumor has it, he was even summoned to entertain a certain member of the Royal Family with the trick – but then again, that could be a bone of contention...

PC world

The road to multiple male orgasms is lined with several options. You could spend years studying the *Kama Sutra*, *Tantric* and *Taoist* scriptures, or you could follow up the tip mentioned in The second coming on page 42. You could risk personal injury (and smash a lot of beer glasses) trying that last trick, or you could start today with the most practical option – exercising your PC muscles.

These are the same pelvic floor muscles, and the same exercises (called Kegels) that women do to tone up vaginally (see Get a grip, page 24). You can identify which muscles they are, by stopping your urine mid-flow. They also enable you to 'lift' your penis when erect, and they contract when you climax – so strengthening them will make your orgasms more powerful.

Not only will you have a firmer erection to wave in her direction, but you'll be able to train yourself to stop on the brink of ejaculation, and enjoy the sensation of an orgasm in your brain, without actually shooting your load. Meaning you can also make love for longer, which coupled with your new super-stiffy, could make you rather popular.

To become a sexual god, first stop the stream of urine mid-flow next time you have a pee. Then continue 'drawing in' these PC muscles and hold for a few seconds (keeping your thigh, back and abdominal muscles relaxed). You're aiming to start with 10 contractions, lasting a couple of seconds each, until you gradually build up to a set of 50 (and by the way once you've identified the muscles involved, the exercise doesn't have to be performed whilst peeing!)

The goal is to do a couple of sets each day, so keep varying the speed to stop yourself getting bored, and whenever you have to queue anywhere, use it as an opportunity to squeeze away. No one will have any idea what you're up to – unless you start showing off in the pub of course...

Made by hand

Giving a great handjob is a skill not to be underestimated. Seeing how a guy pleasures himself will give you an idea of the rhythm and technique he prefers, so whisper that you'd like to watch. Experiment with your grip – being too firm (too soon) may not float his boat, but neither will a feeble stroke that's too soft. The closer you can get to imitating the warmth, snugness and wetness of your vagina the better, so make sure you use lots of saliva, or preferably lubricant for longer-lasting glide.

A fun alternative is to wrap a string of beads loosely around your wrist, and then around his penis (but beware sharp clasps!) How many times you snake them round depends on the size of your necklace (and the size of his equipment) but for maximum ease and effect, roll them up and down his lubed-up shaft with both hands. You could even pop your pearls in the fridge for some added sensory stimulation.

And if your man loves stockings, try slipping one over his erection and ask him to hold it taut. Then slip the other stocking over the first, and start stroking. You should only need the lightest of touches to make him come, as the friction between the stockings creates the sensation. So no tired wrists – and a novel way of recycling any hosiery with holes...

Package deal

Bollocks, nuts, gonads, goolies, plums – call them what you will, but handle with care. A good starting point with your man's balls is to imagine you're cradling eggs (unboiled!) and if he's happy, take it from there. Use flavored lube for a silky smooth fondle, then progress onto licking and 'teabagging' (gently sucking a whole testicle in your mouth).

And whatever you do, don't bite...

“The Penis: aka peenie, love truncheon, weiner, 100% all-beef thermometer, quim wedge, dobber, salty yogurt slinger, wang, beaver cleaver, tummy banana, spam javelin, that thing.”

Chapter 4
Coming to the Point

The word orgasm stems from the Greek 'orgaein', meaning 'to swell' or 'to be excited and lustful'. The dictionary defines it as 'the most intense point during sexual excitement, characterized by extremely pleasurable sensations with involuntary contractions of the genital muscles, accompanied by ejaculation of semen in the male'.

This ejaculation exits the body at 28mph, so it won't lose you any points on your licence, although it is undoubtedly impressive. What's possibly even more amazing, as Jonathan Margolis tells us in *O: The Intimate History of the Orgasm*, is that "in the average lifetime, a man produces 14 gallons of ejaculate, enough to fill the fuel tank of the average-sized family car". Seriously impressive (and a carbon neutral emission).

Us girls don't do so badly either. OK, it might take us longer to get there, but when we do, the results are dramatic. Our climaxes last from 12 to 100 seconds (compared to a man's 10 to 13 seconds) we can have multiple orgasms, and some of us even produce female ejaculate – more of which later.

An intense orgasm can provide a blissful release of mental and physical tension, flooding our systems with oxytocin (the 'bonding' hormone) so we're suffused with feelings of love, warmth and tenderness. Small wonder then that we all strive for the summit, the peak, the 'Big O'. You may know countless ways to enjoy one – or maybe it's something you're not sure you've ever actually experienced (in which case skip this and go immediately to Chapter 5 – Going it Alone).

Wherever you're coming from, here's to your point of no return. May the force be with you.

Cold Feet

A recent orgasm study in the Netherlands found that having cold feet prevented many people from climaxing. Keeping socks on in bed is normally one of the biggest no-no's, but both men and women found it easier to have an orgasm when their feet were warm and toasty. Sales of fluffy bedsocks could rocket…

A little list of Big O benefits (as if you needed one)

1. Forget botox – plenty of orgasms can make us look up to 10 years younger.

2. An orgasm is reputed to be the equivalent in exercise of a vigorous jog, meaning it's giving us a good cardiovascular workout by raising the heart rate, and improving overall muscle tone and circulation.

3. It's been suggested that as frequent male orgasm drains the body of seminal fluid, it can help a man avoid both prostate cancer and congestive prostatitis – inflammation of the prostate gland, caused by prolonged sexual arousal without ejaculation (a condition also known as 'blue balls').

4. Sex is actually a beauty treatment. Scientific tests have revealed that when women make love they produce the hormone oestrogen, which makes hair shiny and keeps skin smooth and glowing.

5. The British Medical Journal has stated that the more orgasms you have, the longer you're likely to live. Apparently men who climax twice a week are half as likely to die prematurely as men who only climax once a month.

6. Feel-good endorphins are released when we climax – reducing anxiety, blood pressure, stress levels and even pain.

“An orgasm a day keeps the doctor away.”

Mae West

Location, location, location

Let's face it, whoever designed the female anatomy needs to go back to the drawing board and move the clitoris down a bit. Granted, there are certain fortunate females who have a very large clitoris, or one that *is* extremely close to their vagina, which can mean they receive enough clitoral stimulation just from the thrusting and grinding of intercourse to enable them to climax. But this is not the case for most women. Extensive research has revealed that only 20% of us climax through penetration alone – and that's because the clitoris (the most common trigger for orgasm) is on the outside, rather than the inside, of the body.

So in a nutshell, the clitoris is where it's at. Big-time. Whether we have a clitoral, vaginal, blended, G-spot, U-spot, A-spot, or a 2-hour-can't-speak-coherently orgasm, you can bet your bottom dollar that the clit is involved somewhere along the line. To quote Ian Kerner in his book *She Comes First* "The clitoris is the powerhouse of pleasure. Any sex therapist will tell you that the number one complaint they hear over and over from women is of an inability to experience orgasm during penis-vagina intercourse... think *clitorally*, rather than *vaginally*... focus on *stimulation* as opposed to *penetration*".

Don't get me wrong, I'm not saying women don't enjoy penetration – far from it – but let's not undervalue the real star of the show.

Not so Grey Anatomy

In the late 19th and early 20th Centuries, it was deemed entirely normal for doctors to stimulate their female patients to orgasm. Sometimes a midwife would assist, but it was mostly well-paid male physicians who aroused ladies to 'paroxysms' in order to relieve their 'hysteria'. So that's what they mean by a good bedside manner...

The second coming

Back in the 60s the ground-breaking American sex researchers, Masters and Johnson, alleged that orgasm and ejaculation were two biologically independent processes, and one could take place without the other. What this means is that multiple climaxes aren't just reserved for the fairer sex – all you men out there can train yourselves to be multi-orgasmic too. You can have amazing orgasms without actually spurting – unless or until you want to. (Also see PC world, page 33).

There is a method for this, with tons of enthusiastic anecdotal evidence to endorse it. We know that massaging the prostate with a finger can enhance a man's orgasm (see Prostate milking, page 89) but taking things a stage further, is the concept of a separate internal or 'male P-Spot' orgasm, which doesn't depend on ejaculation, and is produced by self-massage of the prostate using a stimulator.

There are lots of devices on the market for doing this, but the safest and most effective is the Aneros. It's a simple plastic device, not much bigger than a finger, with a curly T-bar to rest snugly against the perineum (and to avoid any risk of it disappearing upwards). The Aneros was originally invented as a medical massage aid to promote better anorectal health, and it is still partly marketed for prostate muscle toning (it even helps with hemorrhoids). However, it's also now widely enjoyed for its sexual benefits.

Using lots of lube, the Aneros is inserted into the anus, and deep breathing is advised, to allow the body to become accustomed to its presence. The user then controls its movement – not by hand, but by rhythmically contracting and relaxing the sphincter muscles, causing the Aneros to 'stroke' the prostate, which creates deeply satisfying sensations.

Not only are the PC muscles getting exercised – which helps tone the prostate – but with practice, it's possible for men to obtain 'full body', non-ejaculatory (dry) orgasms this way. Best of all, these can last for several minutes, as users learn to 'ride' the orgasm, staying on a plateau that seems to induce what some describe as "a state of bliss". There's no limit as to how many climaxes can be enjoyed, as there's no recovery period needed (and all without batteries!)

There is a leap of faith required here, particularly for straight men, who may at first be wary of inserting anything, but rest assured, this is not so new. In fact it has a history going back thousands of years to *Tantric* and *Tao* wisdom, in which the concept of a higher level of fulfilment (irrespective of sexual orientation) was widely accepted – in a spiritual as well as a sexual context. It's only really new to Western culture, and judging from the level of interest in the comprehensive Aneros website, more and more men are now overcoming their inhibitions and are willing to explore these new horizons.

The penis doesn't even have to come to the party, by the way. It can do – it's possible (and pleasurable) to wear the device during intercourse as it's hands-free, but the prostate is the main player. If you do make love with the Aneros inserted, ejaculation tends to be more profuse as the prostate empties more fully. Devotees also report that they stay harder, last longer, and have better control. The intensely different, earth-shattering orgasm experienced has even been dubbed the 'Super-O'. (What's not to like?)

The road less travelled

It's very easy to become set in one particular way that you know is a fail-safe route to orgasm. There's nothing wrong with identifying your fastest journey time from A to Ecstasy, but have fun experimenting with the B-roads too, finding different strokes and new positions. Sometimes a little detour can be surprisingly rewarding.

How was it for you?

Just about all of us have faked an orgasm during intercourse, and anyone who says they haven't is either incredibly lucky or fibbing! (In fact statistics in a recent UK study found the number of female fibbers to be as high as 80%.) Blokes fake it too, although it's obviously harder for them to disguise the evidence (or lack of it). Women are definitely the main culprits though, and there could be a number of reasons:

1. You want your partner to feel they're great in bed, and you don't want to hurt their feelings, so you're reluctant to admit that you're nowhere near coming in the foreseeable future.

2. You feel like you're 'failing' if you don't have an orgasm.

3. You're exhausted, and maybe if you pretend, then you can get it over with and go to sleep.

4. You're running out of time. The baby's waking up, there's supper to make, and then it's Desperate Housewives...

5. It's been going on so long it's beginning to hurt.

6. You're not sure what a real orgasm feels like – or even if you've ever had one.

7. Because you can. Whether you stage a screaming, face-contorting, Oscar-winning performance, or settle for some heavy breathing and gentle moans, it's not difficult to get away with – but ultimately you're not doing yourself any favors. See the next tip (Coming clean) for some reasons why you shouldn't go there.

“ Sex doesn't always have to end in a climax (for either of you). If you're able to think of sex as being less goal-oriented, sometimes that makes it less intimidating to get things going. Think of it as just having dirty fun (and if you're not having fun, then you're doing it wrong). ” Em & Lo

Coming clean

Faking it is not a great idea. If your partner thinks they're getting it right, and that all it takes is a few frenzied thrusts to transport you to ecstasy, how are they ever going to discover what really works for you? They don't stand a chance of learning to pleasure you properly, and you run the risk of getting locked into a sexual lie that's difficult to get out of.

Not being honest about your needs can only lead to frustration and resentment. Talk to your partner – be open and frank about what you like, but always be sensitive. It might not be an easy conversation, but it's worth it. This needs to be two-way traffic by the way – there may be some things they need to tell you, too!

Don't stop me now

A mistake men often make is to stop stimulating us at the critical moment. When a woman is about to come, it's really important to keep on doing exactly the same thing to her clitoris that's brought her to that point – whether it's with your fingers, tongue or a vibrator. Changing your rhythm or stroke at the eleventh hour can throw us off course, and unfortunately we don't share the same 'orgasmic inevitability' as you!

This tip also goes for girls stimulating guys – although most men do seem to like the action speeded up a little just before they climax, and then slowed right down, or stopped, as they ejaculate.

Women are different. Sometimes we like it if you continue stimulation – very gently – through our orgasmic spasms (and there can be between 3 and 15 of these, gradually subsiding in intensity). Sometimes we might just like a hand cupped gently over our vulvas as we float down from the ceiling. Or then again, maybe we'd like your hand filling the kettle for a coffee. The bottom line is we'll only know what's best if we ask each other and learn to read each other's signals.

“The only time my wife and I had a simultaneous orgasm was when the judge signed the divorce papers.”

Woody Allen

Going with the flow

Female ejaculation is not a myth. It may only be about 10% of women who have the ability to do it – and the jury is still out on exactly what the fluid is – but it certainly isn't an embarrassing display of orgasm-induced incontinence. Clinical analysis has revealed that although it's expelled from the urethra, it is in fact the female equivalent of prostatic fluid. So it's similar to male ejaculate (ie slippery in consistency) but it's clear or only slightly milky in color – and obviously minus the sperm content!

On page 22, Elusive but effusive, I've given details about how to locate your G-spot – considered to generate the type of orgasm that produces female ejaculate. (You can of course have a G-spot orgasm and not ejaculate.) The important thing with all sexual exploration is to avoid putting performance pressure on yourself and just enjoy the learning process.

When the spot is first touched it can be uncomfortable, because you may feel the need to pee, even if you've already emptied your bladder. You won't wet the bed I promise, but for peace of mind you might want to conduct any initial explorations with a towel underneath you. The urge to go to the bathroom will soon be replaced by a deeply satisfying sensation if you continue stimulation.

It helps to be feeling as turned on as possible, as the G-spot swells when it's aroused. It responds well to firm pressure, so start by stroking it gently and build up, using a circular, or a 'come here' beckoning motion, Better still, get your lover to do the massaging, especially if they can go down on you at the same time. It helps to stimulate your clitoris manually whilst using a vibrator specifically designed for G-spot massage – which will guarantee the consistent pressure you need.

If you're making love, the best positions are doggie-style and woman on top. It can be trial and error getting the exact angle for his penis to induce your orgasm – and smaller members are actually better for the purpose. (Told you big isn't always best.)

A G-spot climax can take some time to achieve, but it's worth the wait – it's an extreme, dramatic, limb-tingling experience – whether you ejaculate or not. And if you bear down, pushing your PC muscles out rather than clenching them in just as you're about to come, then you'll increase your chances of squirting – and amazing your significant other. Congratulations! That towel might come in handy after all…

A helping hand

If you're keen to help your woman ejaculate, try stimulating her G-spot quite vigorously. With your palm face down on her pubic bone, keep your index and little fingers pointing straight downwards and your two middle fingers hooked up inside her vagina, then use a firm up and down motion. Make sure she's comfortable with this, use loads of lube, and remember she should 'bear down' as her climax begins.

Thanks for the mammaries

Human females are the only mammals with breasts that jut out when we're not pregnant or breastfeeding – and boy, don't we know it. Fortunately, they are a major erogenous zone for many women (some can even orgasm through nipple stimulation alone) and most enjoy everything from gentle sucking to firm tweaking.

Men enjoy nipple play too – try pinching theirs quite hard, or apply heated lube to nipples and blow for an extra buzz…

“The Breasts: aka dairy arrangements, Bristols, bodacious tatas, norks, dangleberries, rack, plumpies, mildreds, shoulder boulders, Cupid’s kettledrums, baps, coconuts, flight deck.”

Chapter 5

Going it Alone

The word masturbation is derived from the Latin 'manu stuprare', meaning to 'defile with the hand', and up until quite recently the dictionary definition was 'self-abuse'. Back in the 1880s, castration was even performed to remedy this appalling habit, and numerous devices were invented to deter and punish its evil practitioners.

Thankfully we no longer subscribe to the Victorian belief that pleasuring ourselves leads to blindness, madness, genital deformities and nose bleeds (but it is still true, of course, that it causes enormous clumps of black hair to sprout from the palms of our hands).

Hey – get over it. It's a small price to pay for something that feels so great. The official line today is buy some depilatory cream and keep taking yourself in hand – masturbation is good for you. It's the most widely practiced method of safe sex, you don't have to worry about anyone else, and you don't even have to shave your legs – or your palms...(only kidding by the way).

Seriously, it's not just about pleasure, you're in training – to be a more skilled, aware and responsive lover. If you're an expert at making yourself climax, you'll have increased desire (the more sex you have, the more you want) and the knowledge to teach your partner what you like best. You're taking responsibility for your sexual happiness – plus it sure helps you get off to sleep.

Let's not forget Woody Allen's wise words on flying solo – "Don't knock masturbation. It's sex with someone I love." Good on you, Woody. I bet he's got really hairy palms...

Coming into view

Both men and women often complain that partners don't touch them the way they would like to be touched. So masturbate in front of each other if you dare – it takes courage, but it's worth it. You may feel a little embarrassed at first, but what better way of showing each other what you like best, by letting someone witness first-hand how you touch yourself. Not to mention that the sight of you open – in every sense – and losing yourself in your own (normally private) ecstasy is a powerful turn-on in its own right.

Cereal chiller

In1894, Dr. John Harvey Kellogg, an obsessive celibate, invented an anti-masturbatory food designed to take away all sexual desire. The product was called Cornflakes. It's certainly not one of the benefits listed on the packet today, and thankfully no one subscribes to his other dubious theories either.

For little boys, Dr. Kellogg advocated circumcision without anaesthetic, and for the purpose of "allaying abnormal excitement" he recommended "covering the organs with a cage" – whilst for females he advised "the application of pure carbolic acid to the clitoris". Ouch.

It's for you

Hot and horny and stuck at work? Turn off your mailbox setting, put your mobile on vibrate, pop it in your panties and ring it... lots. There's even a saucy iPhone app called MyVibe which is free and tailor-made for the job.

Minge benefits

Shop for some of the less expensive briefs with gussets that aren't sewn down – they make convenient 'envelopes' for slipping phones or compact vibrators into.

Fastest finger first

Let him catch you pleasuring yourself, girls – and having a very nice time. You've carefully orchestrated matters of course, so he 'accidentally' finds you moaning and writhing in ecstasy – and the trick is to be so carried away that you can't stop (i.e. you're a wild, shameless hussy). Bet you any money that once he gets used to the idea, he'll be desperate to join in the fun.

Greased lightning

If you've never tried masturbating with lube before, you are in for one mega-treat, guys.

Any specialist lubricant will do, but for the best sensations, splash out and invest in an oil-based cream. They're made specifically for male masturbation, and they're not recommended with condoms or for vaginas – so she won't try to steal it (like you do with her moisturizer...?)

They're also extremely long-lasting and don't dry out, even if you pump away for hours (as you may well want to when you discover it). Take a look at ID Masturbation Cream – telling it like it is. One user reports, "Second only to the real thing – and sometimes even better". Thanks a bunch!

"Every woman should know how to get herself off. It's an essential life skill that ranks right up there with boiling an egg, writing a resumé, and plucking your eyebrows. At the very least, it's the easiest way to get sex whenever you want it, however you want it."

Em & Lo

A helping hand

Place your forefinger and your middle finger at the top of your outer labia – on either side, so they're in a downward 'V' shape. Then pull them upwards to stretch your inner labia and expose your clitoris – not just for easier access, but because it creates a liberating feeling of being 'opened up'. Keep them there as you masturbate with your other hand, and try this when your lover touches you, too.

Alternatively, some women prefer the feeling of pressing down just above the bikini line – have a play and see which you prefer. Either way, if you're struggling to climax, but just can't seem to get there, giving yourself a helping hand can tip you over the edge.

Sole sensation

This works for both sexes. Try putting the soles of your feet together when you masturbate, so your knees are splayed out to the side. It increases pressure in the groin, making everything even more enjoyable and intensifying your climax.

Wank-a-thon

Europe's first sponsored Masturbate-a-thon was held on August 5th, 2006 in London. Commissioned by Channel 4 Television as part of a series of sex programs, it was also known as the 'Wank-a-thon'. Participants were expected "to masturbate in order to raise money for charity and dispel the shame and taboos that persist around this form of sexual activity".

If you'd like to raise money for good causes but you don't fancy playing with yourself in public, the month of May has now been designated Masturbation Month. So you can pleasure yourself at home to your heart's content – and get everyone to sponsor you into the bargain! It's money for old grope...

Chapter 6

Take your Places

The original erotic self-help manual, the *Kama Sutra*, may be centuries old, but we're still using spin-offs of the 64 positions it teaches – we just don't do the ones that require circus skills to execute, and we tend to give them other names now. (Shame really, a spot of 'suspended congress' sounds rather intriguing.)

I reckon that in reality there are about a dozen basic ways of having nooky that are do-able without making us dissolve into fits of giggles, or feel like we're playing Twister. Here are a few that I think really work – if any are not in your current repertoire and you fancy giving them a go, try them a few times. The first attempt may seem a bit mechanical, but second and third time around you can begin to make them your own, creating your own variations, and things should start to fall into place.

Say it again Sam

With any position, or foreplay, try complementing the action with dirty dialogue – a sort of 'running commentary' on what you're doing – or all the wicked, depraved things you're going to do, if you think that might be well received. Talking during sex can make things über-erotic, especially if you're normally silent. You don't have to use swear words or be a genius with your sentence construction – just start small and whisper dirty nothings in each other's ears. Do it a lot, and certain words or phrases can also become 'triggers' to speed both arousal and orgasm – helping you understand where your partner's coming from (literally).

Dolphins

The man lies on his back with his legs slightly apart. His partner lies on top facing him, with his penis in her and her legs together and straight, between his. She pushes up on her hands, as if doing a press-up, supporting her upper body weight. This way she's able to grind her clitoris against his pubic bone as she slides forward and back on him. Circular gyrating movements work too – or a combination of both.

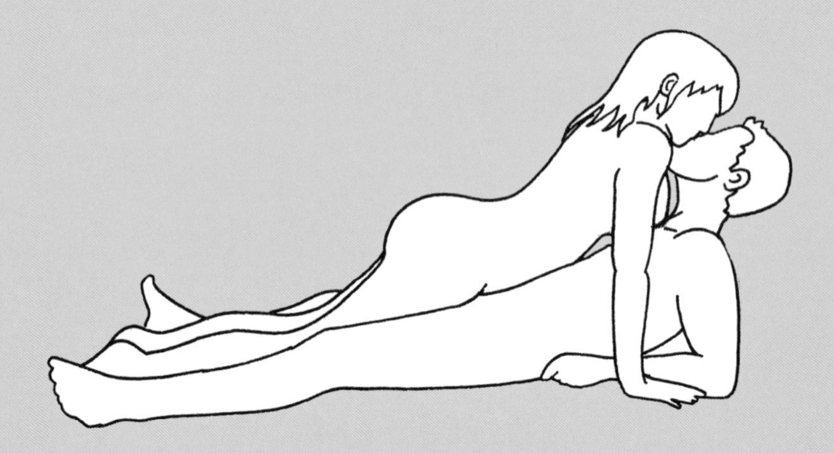

Another variation is to have her legs apart and his together, between hers. Either way the trick is for the woman to use her pubic bone as a kind of pivot – she's in charge and therefore able to give herself maximum stimulation, with the potential for both clitoral and G-spot orgasms.

A fringe benefit for the guy is that he doesn't have much work to do, and a huge fringe benefit for her is that she can rest her body on his, which is a perfect position for those deep, meaningful kisses I banged on about in Chapter 1. After which, you can gaze lovingly into each other's eyes... What do you mean I'm soppy?

Count to 10

This one is good for releasing the animal within you both, but as with all doggie-style positions, vaginal penetration is deep, so if you're well-endowed, you're best to start gently and build up to more energetic thrusting.

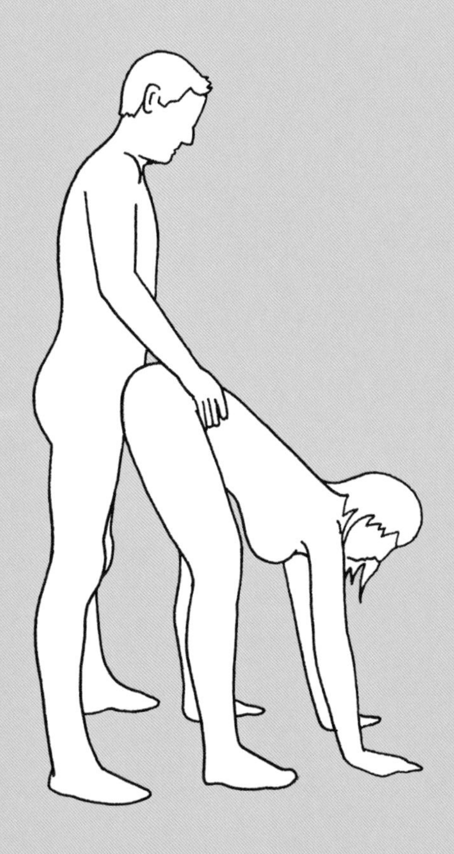

The woman bends forward from the waist, feet apart, knees bent, and with her hands resting flat on the ground. The man stands behind her (she drew the short straw). He then takes hold of her hips and slowly penetrates her, affirming his alpha male status. She is exposed and submissive, whilst Tarzan is totally in control – and enjoying the view. This is a great posture for G-spot stimulation, as his penis is perfectly positioned to hit her hot-spot, and for variety she can move her hands up onto her knees or brace herself against a wall, chair, tree, or whatever offers stable support.

The *Kama Sutra* calls this "the congress of a cow" and advises that "the characteristics of these animals should be manifested by acting like them". Hmm.

I call it 'Count to 10' because with such a visual feast – plus the possibility of fondling your swinging breasts – it's all going to be over in seconds. Moooo…

The eyes have it

To deepen the connection with your partner, try keeping your eyes open during lovemaking. It can feel odd and even intrusive at first – especially witnessing each other's 'orgasm face' – but once you've overcome any initial embarrassment, maintaining eye contact is powerfully erotic and intimate.

Bend me, shape me...

The shower is good for having sex in standing positions, and it's worth experimenting on the stairs too – especially if you have height differences. Bending over the bath is good for rear-entry sex, as is leaning over the kitchen table, or sitting on the edge (with her facing him, whilst he stands). Or if you don't want to move from between the sheets, try adding a little variety by simply swapping sides!

Purr-fect positioning

A good position for maximizing clitoral contact during intercourse is the CAT – or Coital Alignment Technique. It's a variation on the missionary position, but it involves rocking rather than thrusting. The man lies higher up on the woman's body so his pubic bone is pressing against her clitoris to give extra stimulation, and they then practice a gentle rocking rhythm together. Think slow, subtle and sensuous...

Double bubble

Climaxing simultaneously is often considered to be a sensual Holy Grail. As women generally take longer to reach orgasm than men, he should ideally stimulate her (manually, orally or with a vibrator) so she feels on the brink of orgasm before being entered.

Or if it's penetration that does the trick, she could always make him climax with her hand or mouth first, so she can then take her time and call the shots (in every sense) second time around.

Stir your lower chakras

A brief word for anyone thinking of dipping a toe into the exotic – and enlightening – waters of Tantric sex. My previous misconceptions of it involving marathon coupling sessions that only Sting has time for, have given way to a new-found respect. This is an ancient Indian practice that promises increased energy, a sense of well-being, and greater intimacy for couples – physically, emotionally and spiritually.

Tantra (meaning 'woven together' in Sanskrit) believes sex is a life force and a route to heightened awareness. The secret lies in relaxation and sensitivity, rather than the seeking of sensation and stimulation. Orgasm isn't the main focus – it's seen as turning lovemaking into something goal-orientated – so the emphasis is more about a prolonged state of ecstasy, where partners open up and connect without pressure, tension or haste. Foreplay is a priority, for instance the 'caressing breath' (softly blowing over your partner's naked skin) or delicate massage using the lightest of caresses, with fingertips or a feather (the 'erotic touch'). Kissing is also considered very important. Couples begin by sitting down and gazing silently into each other's eyes, gradually letting their breathing slow down and harmonize, so they reach a meditative state together.

'Soft penetration' is practiced too, great for any men with erectile problems. Partners lie on their sides, facing each other and maintaining eye contact, with their legs at right angles and overlapping. As the woman 'milks' the man with her PC muscles, little movement is required, also making it good for anyone with limited mobility. It's surprisingly satisfying.

Then there's the 'Appreciation Ritual', where partners take it in turns to exchange three things they love and admire about each other, or the Yin Yang game, where each lover tries to grant the others wishes for an agreed amount of time.

Enthusiasts say the more they become sensually in tune with their significant other, the greater the trust and benefits in every aspect of their relationship. It's certainly taken the Sting out of Tantric sex for me...

Yawning yoni

This is useful if she's feeling fairly wild and abandoned, and up for showing off her yoni. He gets the erotic thrill of seeing her spread open, plus the added excitement of watching himself disappearing in and out of her wetness. He also gets to drill deep – so it's a good position for smaller penises, as it gives her a more 'full up' feeling.

The woman lies on her back and raises her knees towards her chest. He kneels up against her bottom with his legs parted, and penetrates her, with his hands on her thighs. She can rest her feet against his chest, or on his shoulders, but the closer she draws her knees to her chest, the deeper he'll go, and the bigger he'll feel inside her.

Please note – the higher her legs, the more the stomach is scrunched up and likely to wobble. If she's been overdoing the crisps/wine/Curly Wurlys, then she might feel it necessary to cover her tummy with her hands to hide the evidence. A clever move that not only disguises her innate lack of discipline, but also allows her to press down just above her pubic bone to enhance stimulation. Known in the trade as the Yoni bone-us.

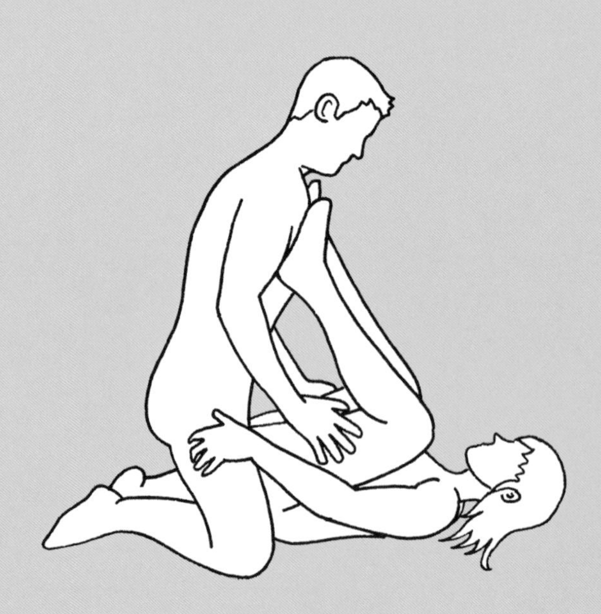

Sensual spoons

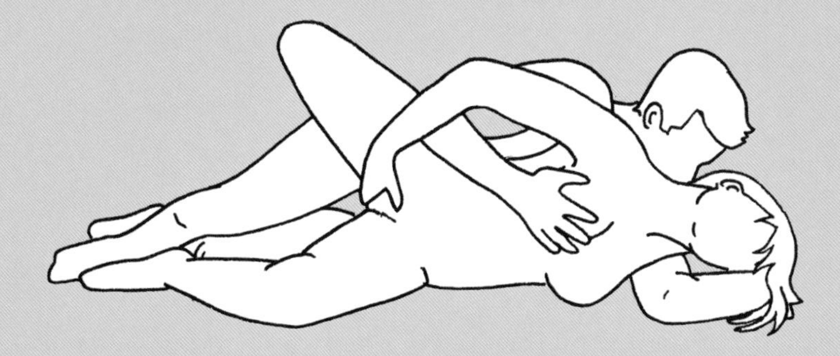

This is a relaxing, comfortable classic, and a favorite for many. Great for lazy sex, sleepy middle of the night sex, or when a woman is pregnant.

She lies on her side, and the man lies on his side behind her – echoing her position, and holding her close. He can stimulate her clitoris, massage her breasts, and cover her neck with kisses – and she can just relish the attention. To make access to her clitoris easier, she can wrap her uppermost leg back over her partners, and pleasure herself – manually or with a vibrator. She can then return his favors by reaching through her legs and stroking his balls – again with her fingers or a vibe.

For a new spin on spoons, try matching your breathing to your partner's, so you're totally in rhythm with each other. Synchronizing your breathing, so you're inhaling and exhaling simultaneously, can bring you closer spiritually, and add a new intimacy and understanding to your lovemaking.

Chapter 7
Tease and Please

Recent statistics state that most women require around 20 minutes to achieve orgasm – a trifle imbalanced when the average man can achieve his in around two. No matter what our differences though, foreplay is the warm-up that works for us all, with benefits reaching far beyond the bedroom. Couples flirt more, they feel cared for, they have a better understanding of what turns each other on – and not just between the sheets.

Be creative with your foreplay. Vary the pace, vary the place. Try warming up in the woods, or some teasing as you watch TV. Begin with a slow sensual massage with some fragrant oil, or wash each other's hair. Cuddle up and watch some upmarket porn (you won't stay at the cuddling stage for long) or read erotic fiction out loud to each other – try Nancy Friday, or the Xcite range of books. You could even have some fun making up your own.

There are hundreds of ways to spice things up – it's really a matter of deciding to. Get inspiration and ideas from erotic movies or literature, and both commit to trying new techniques, positions or sex toys – take it in turns to introduce something new regularly – maybe every month. Prioritize sex in your schedule and have fun surprising each other – let your imagination run wild.

Read on for some more raunchy ideas – it's foreplay Jim, but maybe not as we know it...

You Can Leave Your Hat On

Actually never mind your hat – keep your panties on, though. Whether they're delicate lacy ones, big white schoolgirl knickers or a thong that splits your difference, there's something reminiscent of teenage fumblings that makes this incredibly sexy for you both, not to mention the bonus of added friction. And don't just insist on wearing them during foreplay – yank them aside for penetration, too.

Ring the changes

Variety, said to be the spice of life, can also spice up your sex life. Surprise your partner by daring to be different. If your usual style is soft and gentle, try playing a bit harder and dominating things. Or if your lovemaking is normally more animal, try taking your time with a slow, sensual approach. Don't get into a rut with foreplay either – turn things around; if you generally start with kissing on the mouth, head straight into kissing down south. Just one departure from your usual routine can keep boredom at bay and reap exciting dividends.

Be prepared

Dangerous quickies that carry with them the adrenalin rush from the risk of being caught, are wonderful for adding some heart-pounding thrills to your usual repertoire. Just remember it is illegal to have sex in public, so if you're going to have an alfresco quickie somewhere you shouldn't, think about ways to disguise matters – or a feasible story you can tell if an authority figure rumbles you. "She had something stuck in her throat, officer, and I was dislodging it with this tool" may not totally convince.

New Tricks

If you'd like to try some new stuff in bed, but you're not sure how to broach the subject, try playing this simple game – it'll bring you closer and get you on the same wavelength. Take two pieces of paper and write identical headings on each, such as "My favorite part of your body is... / I like it when you... / I think your fantasy is..." etc. Each of you complete the statements, then swap lists and discuss the results. It should certainly get the ball rolling...

Sex and the Civic

Having sex in a car is not for the fainthearted or the romantic, but it's a surprisingly popular pursuit. In fact 50% of adults in a Durex global survey said it was their favorite location outside of the bedroom. If a stretch limo just happens to be at your disposal, all well and good, but for most it's a choice of his Ford or her Honda Civic. So if you're planning to make out in a motor there are three simple rules to observe, to save you steering feet-first down Cringe Street.

1. **Stop!** Check you've not got company (unless you're into dogging and you get off on having an audience). And it's not a great idea to perform a sexual act whilst your partner is actually driving.

2. **Look!** Be careful to get rid of any incriminating evidence after in-car copulation has occurred, especially if the car's not your own. Clean up any footprints on the windscreen if you were bracing your feet against it, and remember to check for used condoms in the ashtray.

3. **Listen!** Opt for the passenger side or the back seat (in preference to the driver's side) when doing the deed itself. A well-upholstered bottom can inadvertently make contact with the car's horn, which may be a slight giveaway and is guaranteed to cramp your style. You'll be laughing enough as it is.

Practice makes perfect

Try a sexy striptease for your man – you won't look silly if you perform it well, and he'll be too turned on to laugh at you. Move to the Joe Cocker number *You Can Leave Your Hat On*, and study burlesque queen Dita Von Teese to learn the art of removing stockings and suspenders like a pro. Rehearse as much as possible in advance, then dim the lights – and remember to take your time...

Panties by post

If you're working away from home and your lover is missing you between the sheets, give them a treat with an aromatic reminder of you. Package up a pair of your freshly-worn panties and post them (just make sure they go First Class!) This one's not just for the girls either – both sexes love the fresh musk of their partner, and it's a different way to say "Wish you were here".

Wet 'n' wild

The next time your partner is taking a shower, surprise them by joining in – with your clothes on. Actions that abandon practicality in favor of passion can lift you both out of your comfort zone and be an enormous turn-on.

You can ring my bell

Telephone sex can be a powerful aphrodisiac, or a good way of keeping things fuelled if you're parted from your loved one and can only communicate by phone. Speak softly and start slowly by describing to each other what you're wearing, and how you wish he could see you in your skimpy negligée, or how the mere thought of her is making you bulge obscenely, etc. Then build the tension by telling each other what you're doing – and don't spare the details. In fact the more intimate and explicit you dare to be, the greater the turn-on for your lucky listener.

Best of all is that unless you're on a video phone, you can be nestled up in your Winceyette jim-jams/not-so-nice Y-fronts, and no one's any the wiser – just allow your imagination to run riot and let your fingers do the walking...

Meat and greet

Prepare supper starkers – or wearing only a fetching little apron to protect you from hot splashes. Hopefully the sight of you in the buff will produce lots of those anyway, but you'll probably have removed your pinny by then. Men look especially good in those long, stripey, serious chef numbers, with just their bare buns on show.....nice.

Red letter day

Share your fantasies with your partner in a love letter. Using terms you know will arouse them, describe your lovemaking and how much their body and scent excite you. Make it extra special by spraying a little of your own perfume or aftershave on the letter too – our noses are connected to our brain's limbic system, which controls libido.

Sacrificial lingerie

There's something wild and wonderful about tearing each other's clothes off – and I'm talking literally. I once had a memorably lustful exchange with a boyfriend who burst in on me in a theatre dressing room, and ripped open the tight Victorian bodice that was part of my costume. As the twenty-odd tiny fastenings pinged across the room, I did for a nanosecond think what a pain it was going to be sewing them all back on, but this was soon eclipsed by the heady euphoria induced by his wanton, button-popping desire.

That was an unexpected and spontaneous moment, but there's no reason why you can't plan a bodice-ripping scenario. From a practical point of view it's best if buttons and seams are quite loose, so you could use old clothes or lingerie that's on its last legs (which is obviously more economical if you were already thinking of chucking them).

On the other hand, if you feel your tatty old smalls just don't have what it takes anymore, then invest in new stuff, though you may need to loosen some fixings or stitching, so it splits apart more easily. Of course it makes it sexier the more gorgeous you look, but maybe consider undies that are a bit cheaper and flimsier than you'd normally wear – there's no point in buying quality, because it's all going to get torn to shreds in the throes of passion, anyway. That red nylon G-string you got for Christmas may come in handy after all...

Active ingredients

Any type of physical activity (including sex) triggers the release of adrenalin – which then magnifies your senses and makes you more sensitive to sexual stimulation. Taking part in a high-octane sport, screaming your way through a rollercoaster ride, or even watching a scary movie together will get your heart pumping and prime you for passion.

Great sextextations

When I first heard this tip I wasn't very impressed, but I can now say first hand it works – 100%. Send a seriously dirty text (and I'm talking X-rated) to your loved one, and then wait for their shocked reply! It's so unexpected to read a pornographic message on your mobile, rather than "Will be at station in 5 mins" that it really raises the game, and makes you both feel like you're newly together and in lust all over again.

Don't dress for dinner

Go out for a meal and 'forget' to dress. This is obviously best carried out when temperatures are mild, and in a fairly casual restaurant (and wearing the kind of coat that won't look too strange if you keep it on).

When your partner realizes the only thing between them and you is your coat, killer heels and maybe some sexy stockings, there's a strong chance you might not make it to dessert.

All the fun of the feather

Get a feather from an art supplier – or even from a clean feather duster. Then sprinkle a little massage oil over your partner, and watch them writhe with delight as you use the feather to make patterns over their skin. Aromatherapy oils work well too, but make sure you dilute them in a carrier oil first – mandarin is reputed to release inhibitions and ylang ylang is said to heighten sexual arousal.

Little white lie

Take an insider tip from Hollywood heartthrob Cary Grant, "To succeed with the opposite sex, tell her you're impotent. She can't wait to disprove it."

Chapter 8

A Taste of Things to Come

If you want to shine on the sensual stage, it seems there's no better way to win accolades than by being an oral star. A magic tongue will win you a standing ovation every time, so read on for some top oral tips:

For her

1. First and foremost, learn to really love giving him head (or do the finest acting job you're capable of). You'll have no happier audience than your man, as he listens to your appreciative groans while you feast on him. Don't be afraid to be a noisy eater.

2. It's not a lollipop, so don't just lick his penis. Always involve your hands, by sliding one fist up and down the shaft, with a consistent rhythm that begins slowly and builds gradually. Use a confident but comfortable stroke – experiment with several variations – whilst sucking him gently at the same time. Keep your lips covering your teeth, and remember the head of his penis is super-sensitive. Use your other hand to press firmly up against his perineum to massage his prostate from the outside.

3. He needs your mouth, and hand, to be as wet as possible. If your saliva isn't too forthcoming, increase its flow – and his pleasure – by using a flavored lubricant. The juicier the better.

4. For an extra visual thrill, try going down on your knees, a subservient pose many men love. Tie your hair back to give him a better view – and put the spotlight on your skills by leaving the lights on.

For him

1. Make her believe you've got all the time in the world, and you want her to take at least an hour to come. Women are much slower than men, and if we think you're bored or tired, we'll never get there. Ease any pressure, and we'll be beating a path to your door.

2. Take our cue and go very slowly yourself – most women don't enjoy fast and furious, especially at first. Use masses of saliva, licking everywhere else before the clitoris, to drive her mad with desire, and stimulate her with a variety of licks. Make some lazy and flat-tongued, as keeping your tongue pointed throughout can be too intense for us (and tiring for you!) Get her to show you how she'd like it by demonstrating on your palm.

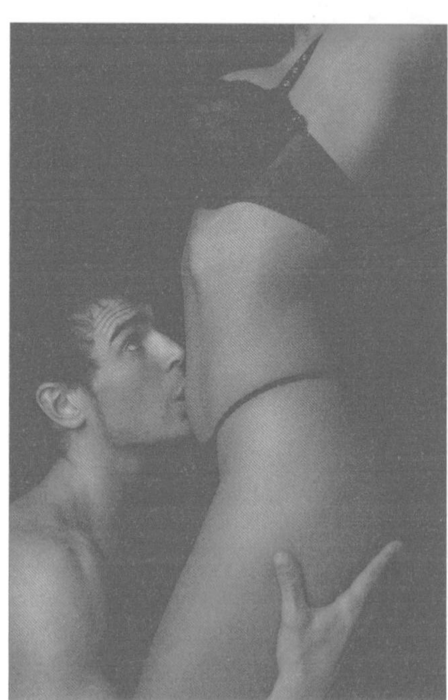

3. Use one or two fingers inside her if she needs some penetration. It can be particularly exciting if you massage her G-spot as you're lapping away, whilst some women may like manual stimulation of their anus. Or both – the 'bowling ball' technique...

4. Tell her how beautiful she is down there and it's driving you crazy seeing her wide open – the confidence she'll feel will make her blossom. Whisper that her smell and taste is really sexy – many of us worry about our girly bits, and a little reassurance goes a long way.

“Researchers have found that oral sex among teenagers has doubled in the last ten years.

So who says there’s no lasting Clinton legacy?”

Jay Leno

What's in it for me?

Semen contains only 5 to 15 calories per ejaculation, a protein content similar to the white of a large egg, and about 60% of the American recommended daily intake for vitamin C. Beats Haliborange any day.

Blow-job eyes

You might feel like you're in a porn movie, but choose a moment to look up at him when you're going down. Holding eye contact a little too long is always a powerful trick to signal desire, and making blow-job eyes when you're between his legs is a clear signal that you enjoy giving, as well as receiving, a little lip service.

The top five things to have in your mouth (as well as each other)

1. **An ice cube** – if you find this difficult, try freezing some grapes or berries – much tastier too. Alternate with bursts of stimulation from a hot (but not boiling) drink, to electrify nerve endings.

2. **Champagne** – the bubbles also stimulate nerve endings, increasing skin sensitivity. Holding both in your mouth isn't the easiest of techniques to master, but sparkling mineral water makes a good cheap alternative until you get the hang of it!

3. **A mint** – the stronger the better. Delivers a fascinating hot/cold sensation that lingers on even after the action has stopped. Peppermint generally favored over Spearmint – or try toothpaste.

4. **Sherbet** – or anything containing it. Explodes in your mouth (as will the recipient).

5. **A tongue piercing** – *only* if carried out by a reputable specialist. Not for the faint-hearted, but if it appeals to you, your oral won't be ordinary. Try freezing your tongue jewelry first, then drinking hot tea, before journeying south.

Gagging for it...

If your enjoyment of giving head is marred by a supersensitive gag reflex, you may find the following advice from the *Men's Health Guide to the Best Sex in the World* rather useful. Dentists have to contend with the gag reflex too, and a recent study reported one technique to minimize it:

"The tooth-torturers gathered the most orally sensitive patients and, using acupuncture or acupressure, stimulated their P-6 regions while simultaneously poking around in their mouths. In the majority of patients the gag reflex diminished considerably.

Okay, you ask, where's the P-6 region? No place too exciting: to find it, put the first three fingers of your hand together and place them, about two thumb widths down, on the inside of her wrist. You press there while she pleasures you, and everybody ought to be happy."

According to traditional Chinese medicine, this is also a recommended treatment for nerves – which may be an added bonus if he's rather large in the dangly department.

Stubble trouble

I'm all for a sexy two-day growth, but it hurts like hell when it's in direct contact with the delicate female vulva (the words sand and paper spring to mind). We love you going down there guys – we just don't want our labia to feel like they've been rubbed back ready for primer and undercoat.

Scheduling in a shave earns you major brownie points, but if you're deeply attached to your designer stubble, or if you sport the full Captain Birdseye, you might like to consider smoothing some hair conditioner on your whiskers before you head south. Leave it on for a few minutes beforehand and we'll be saying "Aye aye, Cap'n" before you know it.

“Do you know the *one* technique that elevates a great blowjob into an outstanding blowjob? Enthusiasm.

More than painting-by-numbers know-how, true oral sex artistry comes from wrapping energy, emotion, joy and rapture into your orgasmic masterpiece.”

Dr. Sadie Allison

The sweet taste of success

If you'd like your partner to swallow, but they don't like the taste, try sweetening your seed by eating strawberries, melon or kiwi fruit, sprinkled with cinnamon. Drinking lots of cranberry or pineapple juice can help too (pineapple is also used in the homeopathic cure for impotence).

You should reduce your intake of curry, cigarettes, coffee, alcohol, salt, and garlic, as these make semen taste bitter and briny, whilst asparagus and dairy products won't do you any favors at all. For a supremely tasty load, try wheatgrass juice – not cheap, but an investment worth making!

Eliminating red-eye

You don't have to swallow if you don't want to – in fact it's definitely advisable *not* to if you don't know your partner's sexual history. Use a flavored condom (or flavored lube on an ordinary condom) then you don't even have the problem. It is however, considered rude and insulting to spit semen out with a horrified grimace, so try having him ejaculate on your body as an erotic alternative.

Shooting over your neck and breasts gives you a 'pearl necklace' to massage in, but if he aims higher, then be careful of 'a shot in the eye' – it stings big-time and causes redness for hours. Of course, wearing glasses gets around this problem – in fact there are entire websites devoted to messing up your specs...

Last night of the hums

Oh, alright – you don't actually have to sing *Land of Hope and Glory* whilst you're feasting on each other, but humming gives both sexes fascinating sensations in the nether regions. The deeper the hum, the more powerful the vibration, and you won't feel quite so daft if you make a sort of "Mmm" sound as you suck, as in "Mmm, this is nice" – which of course it is...

Rolling rubber

Putting a condom on with your mouth deserves serious Brownie points. Unroll a condom slightly and squeeze the air from the tip. Put it in your mouth, with the tip pointing towards your throat and the ring in front of your teeth, keeping them covered with your lips.

Holding your partner's penis, put your mouth over the head, tighten your lips and push down firmly, unrolling the condom as you go. Be careful your teeth don't tear it, and check there are no air pockets (also avoid condoms with spermicide – ugh). Takes practice, but it's a sure-fire crowd pleaser.

Soixante-neuf

The '69' is the most famous position for some mutual oral stimulation, and it definitely ticks the boxes for promoting equality between the sheets. Unfortunately it's often better in theory than in practice. If you lose concentration as you near your happy place, then your partner misses out – and vice-versa.

It's an idea to try lying head to toe on your sides, with a pillow or cushion supporting your heads – or you can just rest on each other's thighs. This is a good position for minimizing neck strain, and it leaves your hands free to help. You can gain better access to each other if both parties keep the top leg bent, with the knee pointing upwards.

Sexpert Suzi Godson has some wise words to add: "The combination of the visual and physical sensations can be extremely erotic during simultaneous oral sex, but to be honest, many people find it difficult to concentrate on their own and their partner's pleasure at the same time. It's a bit like trying to rub your head and pat your stomach at once".

True, but no harm in practicing – I'm all for multi-tasking…

“Oral sex: aka mouth-music, tongue-sushi, playing the piccolo, frenching, lip reading, muff-diving, kneeling at the altar, swallowing the worm, penisuction, yodelling in the canyon (of love).”

Chapter 9
Rear View

The anus has the highest concentration of erotically sensitive nerve endings next to our genitals, and providing you're both in agreement, a foray into some rear action can give intense pleasure, as well as establishing a new level of intimacy. Anal play still carries a taboo tag, but its illicit 'dirtiness' only adds to the thrill. And it's now becoming a more mainstream activity for both sexes, whatever your sexual orientation.

There's a saying that women try anal sex twice – once to see what it's like, and the second time to see if it really was that bad. Witty, but fortunately not accurate. In reality, women get off on the feeling of fullness – in both the anus and vagina, as they share a 'party wall'. And men not only love the tightness of their partner's anal canal, but they're also awakening to the fact that they can enjoy being on the receiving end of some backdoor action themselves, and it doesn't mean they're gay – just enlightened and in touch with their bodies. (Incidentally, the majority of gay men report that oral is their number one sexual activity.)

Remember that our anal sphincter muscles are well practiced at pushing things out, rather than taking things in. We're conditioned from infancy to grip them closed, so when anything is about to invade our bottoms, our response isn't usually 'Dive right in baby, the water's fine'. It requires both a physical and a psychological shift to relax and allow something through, where it's normally one-way traffic. Give your sphincter – and your head – space to adjust.

A bum steer

Some blokes would rather consume a close relative than have you venture into their forbidden territory. Equally, we resent it (understatement) when men claim "Sorry, I got the wrong hole" as they attempt to shove their huge, throbbing, unlubricated member into our sweet, innocent, unlubricated rosebud. Do yourselves a favor by first gauging if your significant other actually fancies the idea – but if that's difficult, you can usually tell if someone's keen by observing their body language.

If you're close to their back door, and your partner arches their back and pushes, or wiggles, their bottom towards you (think monkeys in the zoo) then you're probably heading in the right direction. (On second thoughts, perhaps don't think monkeys.) If they jump out of their skins and yell, chances are your anal advances may not be so welcome.

Seriously – talk it through first, always issue a warning of what your lover is about to receive – and keep things lubricated!

Ring of Confidence

Get your partner relaxed and aroused by first massaging their derrière. Spread their cheeks, softly squeeze them and move them round in circles. Then start gently stimulating the outside of the anus, again in a circular motion, with a well-lubricated finger.

When your partner has started to ease up and trust you, slowly slide your finger a little way in, and if they are comfortable and enjoying the sensation, go a little deeper, still keeping a circular, rather than an in-out motion, to get the anus used to being stretched in this way.

You can try inserting a second finger (but check with them first) and then slide them gently back and forth. Don't withdraw your finger(s) completely, as this is what tends to cause discomfort.

Manicure-cure

You might adore your beautiful lengthy talons, but your partner's anus won't. Long or ragged nails can do some serious damage to the delicate anal tissues. If you can't bear to give them the chop, then wear a pair of latex gloves. You can even buy them in black – not just sexy, but practical too. Try Googling 'Ultrathin black nitrile gloves' and take your pick of suppliers.

They'll make all anal play safe and smooth, and by popping some cotton wool under your nails before putting them on, you'll lessen the chances of them piercing the latex – or anything else. And if your partner is into rubber or latex, a gloved hand job will have them squirming with pleasure.

Rear exit

Never ever make a quick exit anally – with fingers, a penis or a toy. Pull out as slowly and carefully as you went in. The rectum is S-shaped, rather than a straight line, so it's essential to go gently in order not to hit a curve. The sphincter muscles (and there's a double set of them) will involuntarily contract and tense up if you rush things, and your steamy sex session won't have a happy ending.

Dump the anxiety

A lot of people think that just inside the entrance to your bottom lives a load of poo, sitting ready and waiting. Wrong. The manufacture of faeces happens much higher up in the colon – the rectum and anal canal are only passageways, so if our habits are regular, the way is usually clear.

It obviously makes sense to go to the loo before you start, and thoroughly wash and/or use an anal douche or unscented wipes to clean yourself, but venturing where the sun don't shine is a lot less messy than you'd imagine.

“You may be encouraged to know that a recently emptied bowel contains less bacteria than the inside of a human mouth!”

Anne Hooper

Getting in shape

Butt plugs can be useful to train the anal passage and enable either of you to enjoy the feeling of fullness they provide. (They can also be used during masturbation or to enhance conventional intercourse.)

Available in various sizes and materials, they should always be scrutinized for rough edges, as any object for insertion must be smooth to be safe. They're designed to be eased in and then left in place for the session, so make sure they always have a good sized T-bar or flared end, to prevent the very real risk of them being 'swallowed up' – the sphincter muscles are surprisingly powerful.

Start small if you're a beginner, so you don't feel overwhelmed, and use tons of lube – both on the plug and on yourself.

Up at the crack

You can also experiment with 'rimming', which is using your tongue to explore each other anally, also called analingus. Begin by building anticipation, with long teasing licks up from the perineum first. This is the fleshy area between the anus and testicles in men, and the anus and vagina in women, and it's a potential erotic hotbed in its own right.

Some people may like stimulation to stop at the perineum, but if appreciative moans are giving you the signal to continue, then make your tongue as stiff as possible to give the most pleasurable sensations. If you're a bit squeamish or, more importantly, worried about infection, try using a dental dam or a piece of good quality cling-film.

Alternatively, cut open a flavored condom or a latex glove and use those instead. If you choose not to use a barrier, then it's obviously essential to wash thoroughly first, and a good idea when you've finished to rinse your mouth thoroughly with an antibacterial mouthwash.

Prostate milking

Prostate milking refers to the centuries old practice of relieving the build-up of semen by prostate massage. You can still drive him wild today by stimulating his P-spot, more commonly known as the prostate gland, and considered to be the male equivalent of the female G-Spot.

Slowly penetrate him as far as you can, with your longest lubed-up finger – his anus should be lubricated as well. You should be able to locate a small, firm bump on the uppermost side of his anal passage, in the direction of his navel, which has a slightly crinkly texture like a walnut. Press or stroke this P-spot with a rhythmic, beckoning motion (just like for the female G-spot) but be gentle – and make sure it's your finger pad and not your nail, that's making contact.

Some men can be milked to orgasm solely through prostate stimulation. If his penis is waving around and crying out for attention though, suck or stroke it with your other hand to bring him to a powerful, knee-trembling climax, and withdraw your finger very s-l-o-w-l-y when it's all over. (See also The second coming, page 42).

Reach out and touch

You can spice up the missionary position by reaching round and inserting a well-lubricated finger into your man as he thrusts, providing he's up for it – and your arms are long enough! This can be intensely stimulating for him as his orgasm is approaching, and keeping it there will really enhance his climax.

Delve a little deeper

If you're ready to try anal intercourse, then doggie-style (which flattens out the rectum) or spoons is easiest for newbies, followed by missionary, with knees pulled up to the chest – you may find a pillow under your bottom helps too. Straddling him (you on top) means you're in control, which is good, but it does tend to tighten the anal muscles, making penetration more difficult.

Don't forget to stimulate your clitoris to relax and arouse yourself – the more turned-on you are, the easier it will be. Use your hand, or a vibrator if it's easier, and continue stimulation for as long as you need.

Making sure you're both greased to the hilt, ask him to slowly massage your anus with his penis. If you then push out – as if you're trying to have a bowel movement – that will help to relax the outer sphincter and you can then ease yourself onto his penis – there's no thrusting at this stage. Breathe deeply, and once the head of his penis is in, leave it there. Stop and relax for as long as you need to get used to the sensation – the one who's being penetrated calls the shots here, so you set the pace.

When you're ready, ease more of him in, oh-sooo slowly, and then relax around it. If you're comfortable, he can then do some shallow thrusting, or try some gentle rocking, but make sure you're in constant communication so he knows immediately if you're not OK.

Don't worry if you don't manage full insertion at first – you might need a few goes to get the hang of it. It's much more important to be safe, to take your time, and to build up trust between you.

Blowin' in the wind

There's no getting away from it – anal sex can involve wind. If air goes in (as it can with the thrusting motion) it's going to need to come out – another reason to embark on it only with someone you trust and really feel at ease with. You need to know that a fart, if it happens, isn't going to make either of you curl up in paroxysms of embarrassment. It helps, if you're on the receiving end, to go to the loo as soon as you can afterwards, and maybe turn the volume up on the radio if you're worried about any noisy after-effects!

Open sesame (or maybe not)

I'm sorry if this sounds a bit gross, but let's be practical here. If you're planning being on the receiving end of some anal activity in the near future, make sure you get enough roughage in your diet to keep your bowels healthy and clear, but avoid sweetcorn or foods containing lots of seeds, as these tend to remain whole and sometimes overstay their welcome.

As straight-talking American sexperts Em & Lo said in an interview, "One of our favorite tips is to get a daily dose of fiber in your diet, because the more, er, tidy things are back there, the more comfortable you'll be having all your orifices explored".

Some final anal rules

1. Always wear a condom (with the possible exception of monogamous couples who've been fluid-bonded for decades). Anal play is the riskiest transmission route for HIV and other sexually transmitted infections, so penises should always be latex-clad. Pop them on anal toys too – for safety and to make cleaning up easier.

2. Never ever transfer a finger, a penis or a toy from an anus to a vagina without washing it first. They might do it in porn movies, and you might think you'll lose spontaneity if you stop and wash, but your safety is paramount here. No matter how clean your bottom is, anal bacteria can cause nasty infections in the vagina, so don't cross-pollinate.

3. Never use numbing creams for anal sex. It's not in your interest to mask any discomfort, as that can be an important warning signal from your body telling you to take things slowly until it eases up.

4. You can never have too much lube for anal. Take a generous amount – then double it. (Saliva does not count as lubricant by the way…)

Don't even go there…

I suspect every A&E department has witnessed its share of extraordinary items that patients have unfortunately 'sat on by accident'. Chris Gordon in his *Book of Weird Sex* lists numerous bizarre curiosities removed from the male rectum – here's a small selection:

A pair of spectacles, a hard-boiled egg, a teacup, a frozen fish, a torch, a bottle of Mrs. Butterworth's syrup, a sand-filled inner bicycle tube, a 150 watt light bulb, a microwave egg boiler (not in the same back passage as the egg), and a pepper pot labelled "A present from Margate".

“ The Anus: aka mustard pot, back porch, Cadbury channel, tradesmen’s entrance, Grand Canyon, road less travelled, spice island, Bovril bypass. ”

Chapter 10

Fantasies and Fetishes

The biggest erogenous zone we possess is between our ears. The brain is our most potent erotic organ, and plays a central role in our sexual arousal. Indulging in dark, forbidden fantasies can supercharge our sensuality and be an invaluable tool in both masturbation and lovemaking.

It's up to us how mad, bad and dangerous we get – fantasies are about exploring our kinkiest thoughts. There are no rules and regulations, so we shouldn't hold back or be ashamed of our innermost desires – or be disturbed by them. By having wild, illicit role-plays in our heads, we get to imagine all kinds of sleazy scenarios that we wouldn't dream of acting out in real life (well OK, maybe the one about Brad Pitt if you insist).

It's fine to keep a fantasy private, but if we step out of our comfort zone and dare to share, it can revolutionize a relationship, bringing greater intimacy and valuable insights into what turns us on. Pick your moment carefully – suddenly announcing your secret yearning can sometimes be threatening, especially if your partner's left wondering why you didn't trust them enough to let on before.

Pretending you had an erotic dream is often a good way of revealing a fantasy, or weave one into a sexy story you create together. He makes up a sentence, then you do the next… it could even pave the way for some experimental role-playing – if you're both up for it. Don't assume though that just because they love us, our partners instinctively know what we want. And never make fun of each other's revelations. We need courage to come clean – and then we can come dirty.

Quality control

Just like emails on a computer, our mental store of sexual fantasies can get clogged up and stale if we don't do some housekeeping from time to time. Of course, we might have some fantasies that are cherished and special to us, that we need to save for easy access and a shortcut to fulfilment. There are probably some old chestnuts, though, that worked for us years ago but just don't cut the mustard any more.

Re-examine your Inbox and start clearing – to make room for new material that packs a more powerful erotic punch for who you are now.

Colette's tip

If your partner fancies someone else, it's difficult not to feel threatened – but why not bring the third party to bed with you instead? I don't mean literally (unless of course you've all agreed that's an avenue you want to go down, and could handle the consequences).

I mean talk in bed with your partner about the person, what they'd like to do with them, maybe invent a fantasy around them that could involve the three of you. It might be Zac Efron or the girl next door, but it can become your shared secret and even bring you closer – and instead of feeling insecure, you're taking charge.

Three's a crowd?

Think carefully before embarking on a threesome, as they can bring out all the insecurities and jealousies in a relationship. If you decide you do want to experiment – and for many people it's an intensely erotic experience – make sure you both want to, then discuss the ground rules before you find your three-way partner.

Pick someone you can both trust and always use condoms – more people equals more risk.

“The single most potent engine driving sexual desire is our imagination. Fantasies are nature’s built-in aphrodisiac for when your sex-life goes pear-shaped.”

Tracey Cox

Shop till they drop

For some fascinating insights into the field of sexual fantasy, try reading Brett Kahr's *Sex & The Psyche*. Mr. Kahr did some comprehensive research into what goes on – both in people's heads and in their bedrooms.

His findings revealed that 8% of men's, and 5% of women's fantasies involved fetishes. He also concluded that the most popular fetishes were rubber and bondage wear, high heels, boots and fur. Both the sight and feel of sexy clothes – whether it's a miniscule thong or leather basque, red stilettos or thigh-length boots, all have the power to turn us on.

On the other hand...

At least 5% of us never fantasize. But unless your sex life is suffering, it's nothing to worry about. However, if you do want to explore some erotic fantasies, you can get inspiration from various free websites, or check out the frank revelations in Nancy Friday's books. Try to silence your inner censor and discover what works for you – without getting hung up on why.

Come... fly with me

Joining the Mile High Club was a fantasy I'd nursed for years, and I finally got my frequent flyer's box ticked on a long haul trip to New Zealand. A quick word of advice – pick a night flight, and don't attempt membership unless there are plenty of toilets. Go in separately to lessen suspicion, and be as quick as possible – you bent over the loo works well, or him on the closed seat with you on top, facing the door.

It may not be your best sex ever (even though the dip in atmospheric pressure is reputed to increase orgasmic intensity) and the location leaves a lot to be desired. But the illicit excitement of thrusting at forty thousand feet in a shoebox gives you one hell of an adrenalin rush, coupled with the small problem of returning to row twelve without being caught...

Rules and regulations

The Mile High Club actually has an official website and it defines MHC members as "two people engaging in sexual activity (sexual intercourse) at an altitude of no less than 5,280 ft (a mile high above the earth) in an airplane". It has a select celebrity following: John Travolta and his wife Kelly Preston are said to be fans, Janet Jackson and Carmen Electra have sung its praises, and Richard Branson claims to have actually lost his virginity in the air, giving a whole new meaning to 'Virgin Atlantic' (and the expression 'founder member'...) In November 2007, actor Ralph Fiennes underwent some very personal turbulence in the loo of a Qantas flight to India (the stewardess in question was later sacked).

The jury is still out as to whether having sex on a plane is illegal or not. Strictly speaking, a person has committed an offence under UK law, if they have sex in a lavatory to which the public has access (under section 71 of the Sexual Offences Act 2004). However, it does seem to depend on who you're doing it with (preferably not the in-flight attendant) and whether or not you stop doing it when you're asked to. Which is obviously wise.

And don't even think about a post-coital cigarette...

Racy role-play

If you want to act out some fantasies, but you feel self-conscious or just a bit silly, here's a couple of ideas to help you get started. Work out the dynamic you both fancy most – teacher and pupil, master and wench, housewife and builder… and then try scripting a scenario.

Talking through what you'd like to do (and planning appropriate costumes and props) is a turn-on in itself. Then treat it like you're shooting a film – fix a time and be as creative as you dare. Use wigs, make-up, fake tattoos, and whatever equipment is going to make it most real for you.

Body art

If you're considering an erotic piercing (very popular on the fetish scene) always seek out an expert for the job, and follow all after-care instructions to the letter.

Healing time for nipple piercings is roughly 6-8 weeks, and larger breasts tend to heal less quickly than smaller ones. An ice pack (or even a packet of frozen peas) can help relieve soreness, and it's beneficial to bathe nipples daily in a cup of warm salted water. Vitamin C and zinc may help the healing process, but be aware that vitamin C can affect absorption of the Pill, so it's best to take them at different times.

There's a lot of confusion over clitoral piercings; it's far more common (and infinitely less painful) to have the clitoral hood or labia pierced. Piercing the clitoris itself is rare and high risk. Not all women are anatomically suitable for the procedure anyway, as the clitoris needs to be exposed (rather than hooded) and large enough not only to be pierced, but also to support the weight of any jewelry. Plus it can cause nerve damage and permanent loss of sensation in the hands of an unskilled piercer.

It's well worth taking a look at *The Piercing Bible,* a comprehensive and illuminating guide by Elayne Angel, an experienced and respected practitioner.

“Men and women are equally likely to fantasize about sadomasochistic sex, whether giving or receiving. Sexual fantasy is the mind’s way of exploring different parts of yourself, not a judgement on the sex that you’re getting or the partner that you have, or a sign that you’re a pervert.”

Emily Dubberley

Rules of the game

Only play sex games with someone you instinctively trust, and never with someone you've only just met. Spend some time getting to know each other first, and take it from there – if you both want to.

Bondage for beginners

Experiment with bondage by starting with tights or a silk scarf to tie up your partner – whatever's accessible and not too threatening. Avoid pressure points, and never leave someone when they're tied up – or have them tied for longer than half an hour. If any body part goes cold or purple it's a warning sign, so undo all knots immediately. In fact it's a good idea to have some scissors standing by if you weren't in the Scouts or Girl Guides!

Restraining orders

To go a little further with the ties that bind, you can purchase 2 inch (2.5cm) wide purpose-made Bondage Tape that sticks to itself without adhesive. Available in black, pink and several other colors, it forms a secure bond but is painlessly removed – even from hair. Use it to create sexy outfits and to gift-wrap any part of the body.

If you've ever fancied playing 'pass the parcel' with you in the starring role, now's your opportunity...

A bit nippy

Nipple clamps are a popular pain/pleasure toy for both sexes. Build up tolerance with nipple play – teasing, squeezing and pulling – before investing in a set of clips or clamps, and don't wear them for longer than 20 minutes at a time. You can try using clothes pegs before investing in the real thing (stretch the metal spring to lessen the pressure if it hurts too much). Bear in mind too that for women, nipple clamps can feel good or not according to where they are in their menstrual cycle.

Keeping the code

With any BDSM activity (Bondage and Discipline, Dominance and Submission, Sadism and Masochism) or other practices that carry a degree of danger, first decide on a safety or emergency word or phrase, which you both agree will instantly stop the action.

It's clearest if the word you choose is unrelated to sex, for example, "Red" is a popular choice for indicating "Stop right now!" with "Amber" being a warning signal if things are beginning to get uncomfortable.

Saying the actual word "Stop" isn't such a good idea, as pleading for mercy can be part of the fun. You need to have a code word that's not open to any misinterpretation, so if either of you is upset or uncomfortable you can both stop play immediately, without explanation.

Knock three times

If either of you has your mouth covered as part of the game, you'll need a physical sign, such as banging on the floor three times with a hand or foot, to indicate similarly that you want to stop.

Make sure you always have either your mouth or a limb free, to give an agreed stop signal.

Step in time

Foot worship, or podophilia, is a sexual interest in feet and it's one of the most common fetishes. Then of course there's 'retifism' (a passion for shoes) and 'altocalciphilia' (a love of high heels).

The soles of your feet are jam-packed with sweat glands, so they ooze pheromones, which could be what's driving him wild. If your toes are hot to trot why not indulge him and give him a 'foot job' – using only your feet and masses of lube...

Six of the best

For many people, the world of fetishism isn't a game, it's more a way of life. A fetish is the sexual admiration of a specific, often inanimate object, (eg an item of clothing) that becomes associated with erotic gratification, and for some, arousal can become difficult or even impossible without the object being present.

Fetishes can also center around body parts (such as breasts, legs and feet). They can often develop in childhood, when early feelings of sexual arousal happen in the presence of something that may be totally unrelated, but which then goes on to become erotically charged for that person.

The fetish scene has very strict safety guidelines. BDSM relationships are built on trust, and devotees can manipulate their bodily sensations so they experience an endorphin high if pain is administered. If you'd like to dip your toe into a more sexually adventurous arena, here are a few more fetishes to stimulate your imagination…

1. Being whipped – with leather, suede, canes, paddles, etc.
2. Food play – anything from serving sushi (with you as the plate) to messy food fights.
3. Cross-dressing – or just women's underwear – usually worn by heterosexual men.
4. Playing doctors and nurses – enduring various 'medical' play procedures and use of devices.
5. Wearing nappies and enjoying other 'adult baby' practices.
6. Balloon play – 'looners' are aroused by the sight, smell and feel of the squeaky rubber against skin.

According to a Men's Health poll of 2,000 Cosmopolitan readers:

"89 percent of women who have never had kinky sex think it could improve their sex lives.

93 percent of women who tried kinky sex say it did."

Wetting your appetite

Urolagnia – otherwise known as urophilia, golden showers or watersports – is a sexual fetish focussing on urination. It's regarded as one of the more taboo sexual acts, but indulging in something that's perceived as humiliating and dirty gives many people a powerfully erotic release.

There can be an illicit thrill in watching someone pee, or wet their pants (hence the many websites and porn films devoted to the subject) though it seems to be more of a man-watching-woman thing than the other way around!

If it does appeal to you, it's obviously practical to experiment in the bathroom or outdoors – and drinking lots of water or fruit juice will dilute your urine and make it smell sweeter...

Hanky Spanky

Sensual spanking is more about submissive helplessness versus power and control, rather than the pain factor. The most popular position is over the knee (OTK) and the erotic charge is heightened if a specific time is fixed for the 'punishment' or 'discipline' to take place.

Make sure to aim for the 'sweet spot', the fleshiest bit of the bottom where it meets the thighs, and always avoid the kidneys and lower back. Attend to one bum cheek at a time, and if they're rubbed before and after each stroke, it'll build sexual tension whilst also soothing any pain. Take your time, too – a quick succession of slaps isn't so sexy.

Stick to hands, and then purpose-built paddles – or save money and try a plastic spatula or fly swat (test out on your own hand before turning it on your partner). Start with a light touch and go slowly – you can intensify your strokes if and when your partner responds positively.

“While many people find comfort in seeing themselves as ‘vanilla’, pushing the envelope on occasion can revitalize a person’s sex life and open the door to new sensations and pleasures.”

Dr. Yvonne K. Fulbright

Chapter 11

Toys and Playtime

Shopping for sex toys has never been easier. Whether you prefer to buy online, or to be hands-on and handle before buying, there are now sex shops in towns all over the country. Either way, if you're in a relationship, try choosing toys together if you can – it's not only fun, it can be a turn-on too. Plus it's also less threatening for any man who may be in danger of finding a threesome with your new accessory a bit threatening.

If you feel safer just ordering online, there are several excellent companies giving frank and honest customer feedback – and your goodies should arrive in anonymous brown packages (so no blushes as the postman hands you your parcel!) Avoid cheap toys, especially any labelled "for novelty use only" (see A word of warning, page 144) and go for the best quality you can afford.

The range on offer is impressive, with everything from whips to anal beads, lipstick vibrators to I'd-never-get-that-thing-inside-me dildos. Because there's so much on offer, and it can get a little confusing, this chapter contains a few examples that I think are adult toy box essentials…

Prepping up

If you're planning a special session to play with any new toys, have everything that you're going to need close by (maybe even lay it all out the way chefs do with ingredients!) It's a real passion killer having to stop the fun because the lube's in the bathroom, or you need new batteries – if you prepare in advance, you can stay focussed on the job in hand.

The vibrator

There are hundreds of vibrators out there – clitoral bullets, remote-controlled stimulators, finger vibes, curved G-spot vibes, anal ones, awful ones... The choices are endless – in terms of size, speed, material, color, versatility, price, how lifelike, how easy to use, and what's the noise-level? (Meaning will you ever be able to look your neighbors in the eye again?)

Vibrators increase blood flow to our ladybits and boost sensitivity. They have revolutionized the female orgasm – and they've not done too badly for the male one either (his perineum seems to be the favorite hot-spot – the skin between his testicles and his anus).

Apparently it takes an average of 20 minutes for women to climax through masturbation, oral sex, or penetration, but using a vibrator can get us there in anything from 60 seconds to 5 minutes – about the same time it takes to make a coffee, in fact.

No wonder they were the fifth household appliance to be electrified – beaten only by the sewing machine, fan, kettle, and toaster.

Over-powering

A word of warning girls: there's no way I want to spoil anyone's fun (far from it) but beware overuse of your rabbit, bullet, or any other vibrator. Vibes can be addictive, and your – or his – good old trusted finger might begin to lose its appeal after protracted use of a battery-powered friend.

Toys should be an extension of love-play, to add variety, but not to replace the human touch. Take a break from technology for a few weeks, so that your body doesn't become dependent on one route to climax. And then try to combine both methods – mechanical and manual – to give yourself pleasure.

Live wire

For a spot of mutual massage, check out a vibrating cock ring. Made of silicone or rubber, and worn with or without a condom, it's a penile accessory that fits around the base of the shaft, and which sports a tiny vibrating bullet to stimulate the clitoris during intercourse. Not only will it send ripples of pleasure coursing through his manhood, but it'll hit the spot for her too. Enjoy experimenting with positions that maximize clitoral contact – a grinding motion works well.

Two's company

Another toy designed with couples in mind is the We-Vibe. Voted Toy of the Year on Canada's *Talk Sex with Sue Johanson* show, it's a clitoral and G-spot vibrator that can be used alone or worn by a woman during intercourse – which means it delivers throbbing sensations for both partners. Made of medical grade silicone, its innovative design doesn't make it the cheapest toy on the market, but as it's rechargeable, there's no extra expense for batteries. And contrary to what you may think, it still leaves room for him! It's also good for strengthening your Kegel muscles and its clever shape makes it possible to go out with it in place – a pleasantly illicit experience for your nether regions...

Shooting star

Another winner – in the UK Sextoy Awards – is the Tracey Cox Supersex Bullet Vibrator. Not only great value, it's small, stylish, easy to use and incredibly powerful. It's also waterproof and so discreet it doesn't even look – or sound – like a vibrator (it looks, as you might expect, like a bullet). As bullet vibes are tiny, they're great for multiple stimulation and Tracey recommends "holding one alongside your partner's tongue during oral sex". Whichever method you use, it'll take you to your happy place in record time.

Rampant Rabbit – the vital statistics

When the Rabbit made its now legendary appearance in *Sex and the City*, it licensed millions of women to go forth and wave their bunnies in the air. Vibrators were out in the open – no longer something that you hid at the bottom of your knicker drawer. Suddenly everyone was talking about them – even men, who became more cliterate almost overnight.

The Rabbit is now the most famous sex toy in the world. For instance, AnnSummers.com has so many different models of its 'Rampant Rabbit' hopping into our homes, I reckon they must be breeding. Whether you're a bunny fan or not, it's a toy you can't ignore. Meet some of the family:

G-Pulse Remote – Brand new and exclusive, this is the first ever remote controlled rampant rabbit, allowing you to operate your vibrator 'hands-free'.

The Heart Throb – the only vibrator that expands and contracts, so it actually throbs. A combination of ground-breaking technology and skinsoft material – it even sports a diamanté trim.

The Slim Wave – tactile, and with a rippling action that sends waves of pleasure along its shaft.

The Platinum Plus – transparent, futuristic, with seemingly endless speeds, modes and functions.

Aqua – a great entry toy (as it were) for the less experienced. Satisfying, affordable and non-intimidating.

Elite – with breathtaking power to tease, tickle and torment.

Thruster Deluxe – boldly thrusts like no other Rabbit has thrust before.

All have the famous clit-hugging ears, and offer a myriad of vibe permutations – and if you spent a night in with all of them, you might have a bit of difficulty walking the next day. Can't decide which you like best? Guess you'll just have to start all over again. (I know it's hard.)

Sauce material

Lube is a classic bedroom essential, and probably the best, most liberating sex toy in the world. It can enrich every sexual experience by swapping friction for flow. Yet most people associate lubricants only with vaginal dryness or anal sex.

Although it is crucial to use lube for anal sex (as the anus has no natural lubrication of its own) and lube does do wonders for dry spells down below (see Slip slidin' away, page 128) it also enhances masturbation, oral sex, massage, and all play involving toys. Plus it elevates a hand-job from alright to awe-inspiring in a few slick strokes.

Your lube low-down...

Lubricants fall into three basic types: water-based, silicone-based and oil-based.

Water-based feel the most natural – they're the ones that most closely mimic a woman's own juices. They don't stain, they're safe for use with latex condoms and toys, and they rarely cause irritation. They can sometimes dry out if you're going at it like the clappers, but they're quickly revived with a spritz of water or a little saliva, and they're good for both vaginal and anal sex – plus they wash off easily when you've finished playing.

Silicone-based lubes retain their lubricating properties better and longer than water-based ones and they're highly concentrated, so a little goes a long way – meaning they're the favorite for anal sex, as they're thick and latex-friendly. They're oil-free too, so no stains, and they're great for massage (and as a shaving oil – for his chin and her shins!)

Silicone lubes are also completely waterproof, making them ideal for use in showers and hot-tubs. The only downside is that you can't use silicone lubes with silicone toys, because the silicone molecules will eventually rot each other. They're also a little more difficult to clean off than water-based lubes – so be careful not to slip in the bath!

Oil-based lubes are great for anal sex, male foreplay and masturbation. On the plus side, they're very long lasting and never become sticky, but what's not so good is that they're not recommended for vaginal use, and they tend to stain fabrics. Like Vaseline, moisturizers and baby oil, they destroy latex, so along with these, they should never be used with diaphragms or condoms.

So that's a basic run-down. There are lots of manufacturers out there creating exotic variations to add fun and flavor to your new lube-life, including ones in sugar-free, dye-free flavors. If you're juicing up a body part, make sure you warm the lube between the palms of your hands first – much nicer for bare skin than drizzling on cold from the bottle...

There's no excuse for not adding some lube to your toy box – it's not just a woman thing – it can improve both your sex lives across the board. Invest in the smallest size initially, so you can discover what suits you best without spending too much money. Popular websites like www.edenfantasys.com and www.goodvibrations.com in the US, and www.lovehoney.co.uk in the UK, all have great selections. All you've got to do now is think of some ingenious ways to apply your Passion Fruit Punch or your Strawberry and Kiwi... how about popping a bit somewhere on your body, blindfolding your partner, then getting them to search it out with their tongue...?

Labour of lube

It's a good idea to do a skin patch test if you're experimenting with new lubricants – especially the tingling, cooling or warming types. Test your reaction by rubbing a small amount on the inside of your wrist, and use sparingly at first on intimate areas.

If your skin is supersensitive, the safest lubes to use are paraben-free (parabens are the chemical preservatives contained in many products). It's also worth trying those that use plant cellulose as a thickening agent, rather than glycerin or other sugar derivatives which can cause yeast infections.

A little bit of shut-eye...

Buy a special eye mask – or keep one of those issued as a freebie on some flights. Not just useful for a quick snooze, but equally suitable as a sexy blindfold.

If one of our senses is taken away it tends to heighten the others, so now's a good moment for some extra-sensory experimentation. Ask your lover to try stroking you with a feather (deliciously tingly if you can get beyond the tickle-factor) or explore the different ways they can touch and stimulate you. Get them to whisper their most secret fantasies in your ear – it's somehow easier to reveal all when you can't be seen, and very liberating if you both surrender to the experience.

Try this for size

For a new way to enjoy a honeydew melon, guys, scoop out a hole slightly smaller than your willy, then heat the melon briefly in an oven (being extremely careful not to overcook, for obvious reasons). Do a quick safety check for temperature, then add lube before deflowering.

Stiff root vegetables like carrots, parsnips, courgettes, and cucumbers also make convenient, cheap dildos – but make sure you wash them thoroughly to get rid of any pesticides, or peel them if you'd prefer (even cover with a condom for maximum safety).

To paraphrase some sound advice from self-pleasure pioneer, Betty Dodson, "If you're peeling a cucumber, remember to leave some of the skin at the bottom to act as a handle, and don't carve too close to the seeds or your cucumber may lose its erection".

EU regulations are now seeking straight cucumbers with minimum curvature – great for anal or if you like your penetration deep. Brings a whole new meaning to getting your five-a-day...

On the tip of your tongue

If cunnilingus makes you go weak at the knees, then check out The Sqweel – the most innovative sex toy for decades. Launched in 2010 by www.lovehoney.com this oral sex simulator is a rotating wheel of ten soft, chubby, silicone 'tongues' – lapping away at three different speeds to tease, please, and finally induce a knee-trembling climax.

Lube is required, but a man isn't – this is incredibly life-like. Close the windows, turn off the phone, and get ready to squeal...

I-scream!

The Cone is the modern-day equivalent of that old favorite, the spin cycle on a washing machine – except in compact form that's a bit easier to transport. (Having said that, it's not exactly a discreet little number that you pop in your wash bag, hoping it'll go unnoticed).

As vibrators go, it's a big one, but it needs to be – it's hands-free and sits solidly on the floor, so you can squirm around happily on its point. You can then take yourself through each of its 16 pulsating, vibrating settings, and if you get impatient, just press the shortcut 'Orgasm Button' (one thing my washing machine doesn't have).

It was originally designed as part of an S&M chair, but apparently proved to be far too comfortable for pain lovers. There's a big buzz about this one – literally – but a lot of it is muffled when you're sitting on it, and I haven't had so many laughs with a toy in ages. A vibrator that puts you in the driving seat.

Sunny side up

For the ultimate party in your pants try a remote controlled egg-shaped vibrator. Invest in one that's suitable for both external and internal stimulation and manage the hands-free control yourself – or let your partner decide when to drive you into a frenzy of egg-citement.

“Check your lubricant before you play with your toys. Silicone-based lube erodes silicone toys, and oil-based lubes will erode latex condoms, which some people use to cover their toys. A water-based lube works with everything.”

Scarlet magazine

Silence is golden

Noise is something most of us worry about – especially in a shared house. It is possible to get a very quiet vibe, but you might have to forfeit some other functions and it may not be as powerful. Turning your music up usually works quite well – or camouflage the buzz by adding an extra layer or two of bedding. If you're still worried, you can always use your vibe in the bathroom and pretend it's an electric shaver/toothbrush…

Massage meltdown

According to a recent Durex survey, 54% of women think massage is the best method of seduction – so why not give it a try?

It's not difficult to give a soothing and sensual massage, even if you're inexperienced. Be guided by your partner as to what feels good for them, and for safety, don't work directly on the spine or dig into muscles too deeply – use a gentle or medium pressure.

If your hands are on the rough side, then wearing thin non-latex gloves (available from pharmacies) will mask any callouses – and give a totally different sensation into the bargain. Experiment using different objects too: trail some chiffon or velvet across shoulders, or try swirling a plump makeup brush around the backs of knees.

Playing clean

Non-porous toys, made from stainless steel, glass, or medical grade silicone, are the easiest to sterilize. Try the dishwasher if there are no motorized parts, otherwise use a specialist product – or wash them carefully with antibacterial soap and water, letting them dry naturally (and make sure they're completely dry before storing).

Slip a condom over toys made from other materials – and throw away any that are scratched or damaged, as they're a breeding ground for bacteria.

Gender-bender

Strap-ons are becoming increasingly popular – they always have been in the world of girl-on-girl sex, but now there's a new phenomenon of couples wanting to try female to male penetration. It's sometimes called 'pegging' (don't ask me why) and one of the specialist dildos to hit the headlines is the eye-watering Tantus Feeldoe Vibrating Double Dildo. Quite a mouthful, in more ways than one.

A strap-on can look strangely thrilling on a woman, even if it's just for show. Normally the woman has to wear a harness or specially designed pants to keep the dildo in place, but this one doesn't need either – the wearer fits the smaller bulbous end of it into her vagina, leaving the dildo protruding (think bendy straw with the long bit shaped like a penis). You need powerful PC muscles to do the job of keeping it there – and if they're not powerful now, they sure as hell soon will be!

On page 90, Delve a little deeper, I give practical guidelines on anal intercourse, all of which applies to pegging too – but do make sure you use loads of thick, water-based lubricant (silicone-based lubes destroy silicone toys).

Feeldoe was designed by a woman, for women – which is why it is wisely designed in a choice of three sizes. It also has little ridges thoughtfully positioned to give the wearer clitoral stimulation, whilst both parties can relish the skin-on-skin intimacy it offers. This might not be for everyone, but for a lot of women – and men – it's a huge turn-on. It's about the closest a girl can get to having a willy, without growing her own.

A man's best friend

Male sex toys are sometimes accused of appearing slightly gross, but Japan has a gift for the guys that is both stylish and discreet. The Tenga Flip Hole is a state-of-the-art masturbation device for men which is so futuristic looking, you'd be forgiven for thinking it's the latest accessory for your iPod. The casing conceals a jelly-like silicone sleeve, moulded to give lifelike sensations, with three buttons offering different sensations for your shaft. It massages, squeezes and sucks – and to make you feel really at home, it even makes sexy little slurpy noises as it pleasures you.

Reusable, easy to clean, no batteries – and it never gets a headache.

Classy glass

Dildos have been around for centuries and glass dildos offer a very different sensation from rubber or silicone varieties. Most glass dildos are now made from high-grade pyrex which is safe, sturdy, super-smooth and obviously designed not to break inside you – even if you have turbo-charged pelvic floor muscles.

They can be heated under the tap or chilled in the fridge to give even more tantalizing thrills – plus they're easy to clean and recyclable (not that you'll want to throw it away).

Pass go and collect...

If you're secretly yearning to put that hotel down on Mayfair, but it's not your loved one's idea of a fun night in, dim the lights and set up instead for a steamy game of Monogamy – A Hot Affair... With Your Partner!

Voted 'Adult Game of the Year', it's packed with raunchy, inventive ideas to inject excitement and desire into a relationship. It's full of surprises and humor too, in fact it's quite an eye-opener – however well you think you know each other! And just like Monopoly, you might not make it to the end...

Little...

A good friend of mine has always extolled the virtues of the electric toothbrush as an aid to self-gratification. It's now gone official as a legitimate sexcessory in the shape of a pert little gadget called Tingletip, which looks just like a toothbrush head (but thankfully without the bristles).

Blessed with a unique contra-rotating action, its vibrations are intense for something so tiny, and because of its innocent, almost clinical appearance, you could easily pass it off as a gum massager (so minimum embarrassment if it's a travelling companion and your suitcase is searched at the airport).

The only downside is that electric toothbrushes are a bit noisy – but then so will you be.

...And Large

No toy collection is complete without the legendary Hitachi Magic Wand. Introduced in the 70s as a medical massage device, it is still wonderful for aching backs, but it's also capable of rendering you speechless when it comes to more private parts of the anatomy. It's reassuringly non-sexual in appearance, and a little on the loud side if I'm being really picky, but the orgasms it delivers are as good as it gets.

Our nerve endings gradually deteriorate due to ageing and lifestyle, so more vibration is needed as we get older, making this a particularly good toy for the more mature woman – it's always been the weapon of choice for US sexual pioneer Betty Dodson, now in her eighties and still going strong.

The Magic Wand is mains powered, so it's pretty insistent (to say the least). In fact, it just won't take no for an answer...

Chapter 12
Trouble Shooting?

There are certain times in everyone's lives when body parts refuse to co-operate. It's frustrating when they're attached to you and they were working just fine yesterday, but if we don't panic, they often put themselves right, and we're only left with a little dented pride. For example, 60% of men over the age of 35 experience erectile problems at some stage, and scores of women lose their libido because of stress, tiredness, low self-esteem, or a whole combination of reasons.

Problems can arise with long-term relationships when the initial novelty wears off – libido often fades with familiarity, and desire is no longer a given. Successful long-term sex is fuelled by a mixture of effort, intimacy and imagination – all blended together with the magic ingredient of time. That's something most of us have in short supply, but if we use it wisely and are supportive and patient with each other, we can salvage an ailing sex life. There's no substitute for talking things through openly and honestly – a good starting point might be "What can I do to make things work?"

If your sex life seems to have dwindled away completely, it's worth scheduling in some lovemaking sessions which you both stick to. Don't worry about the lack of spontaneity – the anticipation of your date can be great foreplay in itself. And make love even if you don't feel like it. As Michelle Weiner-Davis, author of *The Sex-Starved Marriage* says, "Sometimes the hardest part of running is putting on your shoes. So just do it".

Korma chameleon

If your man falls asleep immediately after sex, don't take it too personally – he's only succumbing to biological forces. When a man ejaculates, he releases several hormones that encourage relaxation and sleep. Short of transforming yourself into a take-away curry, there's not a lot you can do – although getting him to breathe more deeply during lovemaking may oxygenate his system, and help him stay awake longer.

Cold comfort

Sometimes you can be best friends – you laugh, chat, use nicknames – but any passion in the bedroom is long gone. Being so close and comfortable together is lovely, but perversely, cosiness can be counter-productive to passion, because the sense of danger has disappeared.

Re-awaken your ardour by planning some raunchy surprises for each other – unexpected locations, sex toys and acting out fantasies can all help, but start by banning those nicknames from the bedroom. Let's face it, "Mr. Wibbly Wobbly" just isn't going to be the man to roger you senseless..."

S-exert yourself

A visit to the gym can boost a flagging libido. Studies have shown that just thirty minutes a day of exercise can help increase our sex drive. Exercise pumps blood around the whole body, crucial for arousal. It also stimulates the endocrine glands – meaning raised testosterone levels (which stimulates desire in women as well as men). Plus if you feel more confident about your body, you'll feel sexier too.

Does my bum look big in this?

Interestingly, men are far less focussed on a woman's physical faults than we are ourselves. They really don't scrutinize our cellulite bottoms the way we do. Try not to obsess about wobbles – or whatever worries you – as that can be a turn-off in itself.

Ring me...

If your penis loses the plot in the middle of the action, you may find help in the form of a penile constrictor ring, worn around the base of the shaft. They convert a weak erection into a strong one by enhancing blood flow, and can also delay ejaculation. But never wear them for more than 30 minutes at a time, and don't use if you're diabetic, have circulatory problems, or you're on any anticoagulant medication – including aspirin.

Choose carefully, as one that's too small runs the risk of getting stuck (so flexible silicone is better for beginners than a metal or leather cock ring) and lube up first for easy removal. You may find it helpful to trim or shave some of your pubic hair on the scrotum and around the base of the penis, to prevent painful pulling.

Some guys may prefer to adorn their tackle with a ring that embraces the balls as well. Try putting it on before you're erect – it's much easier, and you can savor the feeling of tightness as you get hard.

DIY SOS

The female genitals are their own self-cleaning eco-system. More hygienic than many other parts of the body, including the mouth, they've been described as being as healthy as a carton of yoghurt!

This might seem an odd comparison, but the kind of healthy bacteria found in yoghurt – lactobacilli – are also present in vaginal secretions, which is why eating natural, unsweetened yoghurt can help stave off vaginal infections, or restore the correct balance when an infection is present.

And there's more than one way of taking it – try putting some on a panty-liner at bedtime to ease the symptoms of thrush. Just make sure it's the plain, unflavored variety containing live cultures (mandarin orange might seem more appealing, but it won't do the trick!)

Speed limits

Premature ejaculation is one of the most common problems experienced by men, but it can be successfully cured by squeezing the penis just below the head when you're close to coming, or by stopping thrusting the moment you feel your orgasm approaching – and then pausing before continuing. Try using this stop/start technique when masturbating too, along with visualizing deeply unsexy images. Learning to control your orgasms like this during masturbation can benefit your lovemaking with a partner.

You can also use a condom like 'Extended Pleasure' by Trojan, which contains a tiny amount of local anaesthetic (benzocaine) in the tip. This desensitizes the penis head, so intercourse can last longer.

Scent of a woman

Every woman has her own unique taste and scent – her own aromatic signature. It's well-known that Napoleon used to prefer Josephine when she was a little savory ("Don't wash, I'm coming home" was a favorite command) and healthy female love juices are a considerable turn-on for most men.

However, if you're washing regularly but you're conscious of a bad or unnaturally pungent genital smell, do check it out with your doctor or clinic to make sure there aren't any underlying medical issues. If you're OK but the problem continues, take a look at your diet and lifestyle; stress, heavy drinking, smoking, and a lot of spicy, animal or dairy products can all affect us vaginally (basically the same foods that influence our breath and body odor).

Avoid any lubes or body lotions that are petroleum-based as they can clog you up, and so-called 'intimate' sprays or scented douches can not only disrupt our natural balance of flora and fauna, but also disguise our own inherent musk. You could end up smelling more like a cleaning product than a person – not the desired effect.

O-MG!

Hailed by some as the "greatest news for women", Durex Play O is an orgasm-enhancing gel that works by encouraging blood flow to our most sensitive area. It's applied to the clitoris just before the fun starts, and claims to help women not only orgasm, but to experience the most intense orgasm they've ever had.

It's the only stimulating gel to use flavors instead of menthol to create its tingling effect. And tingle it does – within minutes you'll be feeling hot and bothered (in the nicest possible way). That ticks the libido-lifting box then, and the little frosted bottle doesn't scream sex, so it wouldn't raise an eyebrow if spotted on the bathroom shelf. It may be small, but a little goes a long way…

Can't come, won't come?

If you're a bloke who's having trouble ejaculating during intercourse, but the problem doesn't occur when you're masturbating, it may be to do with the way you're actually pleasuring yourself. If your technique is to squeeze your penis hard, or stroke it really fast, a vagina isn't ever going to match up to what your hand can achieve. You need to re-educate your organ to respond to a far lighter touch. Postpone masturbating for as long as you can manage, then when you do, stroke yourself softly and slowly, using only your fingertips and maybe a little lubricant. This should gradually make you more sensitive when it comes to intercourse – and hopefully the next time you make love should be explosive…

Partners in porn

If your partner is into porn and it's stressing you out, explain how redundant it's making you feel, and that you want a share in the fun. Be more assertive sexually – ask if there's something you can watch together, and tempt him visually by wandering around scantily clad or naked. One of the reasons men enjoy porn is because it's an easy, speedy fix, so instigate some sexy quickies sometimes as a change from longer lovemaking sessions.

Slip slidin' away

Many factors can cause vaginal dryness – it's a very common condition. Just because you're not wet, it doesn't mean you're not interested. It's also possible to be dripping one minute and then dry the next (this often happens after climaxing).

The amount of natural lubrication a woman produces varies according to oestrogen levels, and can be affected by your menstrual cycle, childbirth, breastfeeding or the menopause. As a woman matures, it also takes longer for her to become aroused, and her lubrication is not so acidic (which can make her more susceptible to vaginal and urinary tract infections, such as cystitis). Medications like antihistamines, antidepressants and the Pill, together with your stress levels and how much you drink and smoke, can also have an influence.

Adding saliva to your own juices is a help, but spit dries out quickly when it's exposed to air, so keep a glass of water nearby to moisten your mouth. Better still, invest in one of the umpteen specially formulated personal lubricants now on the market – these can transform painful intercourse into slippery bliss, and they're great for pleasuring both of you. Turn yourself into dessert with Sliquid Swirl's 'Green Apple Tart' (an Oprah favorite – from Drugstore.com) or the BabeLicious range of lubes from Babeland.com – dulce de leche, mojito peppermint, and pomegranate vanilla. Yummy. (Also see Sauce Material, page 113.)

Flushed with success

The easiest way to prevent an attack of so-called 'honeymoon' cystitis, is to have a pee as soon as possible after intercourse. This helps to flush away any germs, and you may also find it comforting to gently wipe yourself (always from front to back) with a clean, warm facecloth. Also use lubricant during sex to avoid any potential bruising of delicate tissues, and drink cranberry juice – believed to help stop bacteria sticking to the urinary tract.

Viagra... the low-down

Age is no barrier to using PDE-5 inhibitors – the clinical name for Viagra, Levitra and Cialis. They don't create desire, but they should help with the hydraulics – whatever your age.

What *is* a barrier, though, is that men who are already taking nitrate-based medicines must steer well clear. Viagra works by relaxing the blood vessels, so an erection is facilitated by more blood flowing to the penis. However, if combined with other drugs also designed to relax blood vessels (such as Nitroglycerin, used in treating heart conditions) then blood pressure can drop to life-threatening levels. Always get Viagra from a doctor who can look at your overall health picture (there may be other factors contributing to erectile dysfunction) and never risk buying it online.

The commonest side-effects are headaches, stomach upsets, dizziness, facial flushing, nasal congestion and blurred vision. Some users report seeing a 'bluish tinge' for several hours, and interestingly, it's because Viagra can cause color vision problems that pilots can't take it within 12 hours of flying.

Cialis works faster than Viagra or Levitra (which are both taken about an hour before intercourse, with their effects lasting 4-5 hours). Cialis produces results after only 20 minutes, and it lasts for 36 hours – hence its nickname 'The Weekend'. (You can take it on Friday night and still be up for action – literally – on Sunday morning.)

Pumping iron

One alternative to taking medications like Viagra is to use a vacuum pump: a cylinder is fitted over the penis and within minutes a manual or motorized pump creates an erection-inducing vacuum, whilst a ring around the base of the penis keeps things firm for about 30 minutes. Pumps might lack spontaneity but they're inexpensive, available without visiting your doctor, and if used carefully, have no side effects.

Relight my fire

Our sexual appetite varies throughout our lives, and although society is far more comfortable with sex under the age of 50, our need for intimacy doesn't usually disappear as we get older. It's perfectly possible to enjoy a fulfilling love life well into our 50s, 60s, 70s and beyond.

It's true that more of a conscious effort is needed to maximize enjoyment. The menopause can cause emotional as well as physical changes, so women may feel less receptive to their partner's advances, take longer to become aroused, become bored with bedroom routine, or find that medications and physical wear and tear can affect desire.

This goes for men too, of course, who can find that their ability to have psychogenic erections (brought on simply by erotic thoughts or images) decreases with age. Bear in mind though, that it's always wise to check out any erectile problems with your doctor, as they can also be an early sign of other health issues.

Try jump-starting your libido with some sensual treats – the trick is to be creative, have fun, and have a few surprises up your sleeve. Enjoy a fragrant, candlelit bath together, followed by a luxurious massage with some aromatic oil. Snuggle up on the sofa and watch an erotic movie (try *The Secretary* for starters) or have a slow romantic dance to some old favorites. Tempt each other visually with some new, inviting undies, and make your bedroom more romantic with soft, flattering lighting and crisp, clean sheets. And if you normally make love at night, consider switching to the morning – levels of testosterone, the male sex hormone, are highest then, so mornings may be the best time for him.

Reconnect to your sensuality and put sex back on the agenda – you'll find that the more you have, the more you'll want.

“Because our society puts so much emphasis on the young, the truth that older people have sex and enjoy it tends to get overlooked. In fact… there’s an undercurrent of belief that older people having sex is icky, maybe even something that shouldn’t be done.

If you buy into the assumption you should be sexless, then that’s going to diminish your sexuality. Young people are pushed towards having sex before they want to, in part because of peer pressure, and older people end up being pushed away from having sex, because of society’s attitude.

We’re all sexual beings and we should admit it. Sex can bring great benefits, and you deserve them no matter what your age.”

Dr. Ruth K. Westheimer

Chapter 13
Nature's Helpers

Named after Aphrodite, the Greek goddess of love, an aphrodisiac is something that claims to arouse or increase sexual desire. Almost anything can have aphrodisiac qualities, but we generally think of them as being something that you eat or drink. They can also be used to improve your performance, or to ward off exhaustion if you intend banging away all night.

Wholesome nourishing foods such as shellfish, honey, eggs, seeds and nuts have traditionally been regarded as the most reliable stimulants – possibly because they compensated for a nutrient-poor diet in some cultures. Aphrodisiacs were also believed to increase fertility, and thought to have sensual powers because of their smell, texture or shape. An open fig can resemble a woman's vulva, an oyster can feel or smell like male and female love juices, and bananas, carrots, eels and asparagus all have an obviously phallic appearance.

If you're thinking of experimenting with some of Nature's helpers, remember that the very act of preparing treats for someone and 'setting the scene' is in itself a loving gesture. We can enhance our erotic enjoyment by appealing to all our senses – lighting, fragrance, music, and a relaxing atmosphere can all contribute. Try abandoning the cutlery and feeding each other with your fingers too – so much sexier.

Exploring aphrodisiacs, whether they're folklore or fact, can be a catalyst for added excitement in a relationship – and I bet you'll have a few laughs in the process. Who cares if they're a myth – so long as they add a little magic.

Girl talk

I've always loved that old joke "What do you put behind your ears to attract the men? Answer: your ankles…" On a more serious note though, if you're very comfortable with your own scent, your personal 'cassolette' (the French term for your own intimate smell) there's something very exciting for your mate if you dab a little of yourself behind your ears. Forget expensive perfume, a little bit of unique, pheromone-packed 'Me No. 5' can go a long way – plus it's free and always to hand!

Goat for it…

A herbal supplement that deserves a mention is the aptly-named Horny Goat Weed – christened centuries ago by a Chinese goat herder, who noticed that his rampant goats couldn't keep their hooves off each other whenever they chewed a certain weed. Used for over 2,000 years in Asia as a traditional remedy for liver, kidney and joint disorders, it's gained a reputation in the West as a sexual cure-all and carnal firecracker.

Willy vanilly

Vanilla has long been regarded as a sensual stimulant. The sex researcher, Havelock Ellis, made the discovery that employees in a vanilla pod factory were in a constant state of lewd arousal – apparently its aroma increases blood flow to the penis by 8%.

Good job they weren't harvesting lavender – a whiff of that accounts for a sizeable 18% engorgement in the male nether regions… what a waste to keep that sachet scenting your drawers.

“Erection is chiefly caused by parsnips.”

Aristotle

The old ones...

The *Kama Sutra* offers a recipe that claims to make the reader "strong for the act of love and disposed to lying together". It suggests a goat's or ram's testicle boiled in sweetened milk, served with buttered, honeyed rice, and a side dish of sparrows' eggs. Legend has it that Aphrodite considered sparrows to be sacred because of their "amorous nature", and for that reason they were often an ingredient in various erotic brews.

...are maybe not the best

While a recipe from *The Perfumed Garden*, a 16th Century Arabic treatise, recommends a glass of very thick honey, with 100 pine nuts and 20 almonds, to be taken for three nights at bedtime. Just make sure you also book an appointment with your dentist.

Sow your wild oats

Testosterone is a powerful hormone responsible for libido and performance, in women as well as men. Oatmeal is thought to help release and activate it, as wild oats contain an enzyme that frees up 'bound' testosterone in the body – with women reporting an increased sex drive and men displaying firmer erections. The three bears certainly knew what was good for them, so make porridge, muesli or oatcakes part of your daily diet.

Ready heady go!

Certain essential oils are reputed to be sexually stimulating (our noses are connected to our brain's limbic system, which controls libido) so pop some drops into a bath and take a soak – preferably with your partner. Try jasmine, ylang ylang, rose, sandalwood and juniper to really get you in the mood (either separately or as a cocktail) or add a few drops to a neutral massage oil for some seriously sensual stroking.

Sin and tonic

An ancient energy-giver that's still going strong is ginseng. For centuries, men in Asia have been using it to boost their sexual performance, increase stamina, and treat erectile dysfunction. The word literally means 'man root' and – aside from its uncanny resemblance to the human body – recent tests in China show that it also increases testosterone in both sexes as well as being a powerful, rejuvenating tonic. So go grab that ginseng, especially the potent Red Korean variety. You won't grow a beard, girls – and you'll be dynamite between the sheets.

Wine wisdom

A moderate quantity of wine is thought to have an aphrodisiac effect. Opinions differ as to whether red or white works better, so the obvious thing is to follow your preference.

Choose quality over quantity though, as too much alcohol of any kind can leave you grinding to a flaccid halt. Drink enough to loosen inhibitions (and clothing) and then stop before sleep starts to seem like a preferable option…

Herbal viagra?

Muira Puama is a herbal stimulant extracted from the roots and bark of the rainforest trees in Brazil – in fact it's called 'potency wood' in South America because of the punch it packs. Dr. Jacques Waynberg, from the Institute of Sexology in Paris, has found it to be effective for attaining and maintaining an erection by increasing blood flow to the penis, and for reviving sexually jaded appetites in both sexes – so it helps psychologically as well as physically. It's also used for staving off rheumatism and baldness, making it one very versatile herb!

Pearing off

The Aztecs called the avocado tree 'Ahuacuatl' meaning 'testicle tree' and avocados were thought to be so potent that, in the words of Cynthia Watson MD, the Aztec culture "forbade village maidens to set one virginal toe outside the house while the fruit was being gathered". It's true, avocados do resemble a pair of testicles when they're hanging in pairs on the tree, but there's much more to them than meets the eye. Not only are they delicious, they're also packed with folic acid, vitamin B6 and potassium, giving you both energy and a libido lift. Try some balsamic vinegar on their slippery flesh – eat them with your hands, then lick it off each other's fingers...

Coming to the crunch

It may not seem an obvious aphrodisiac, but celery can really get things going. It contains androsterone, a hormone released by men when they sweat, and it's a considerable turn-on for women. So don't dodge the salad, boys – this one is said to give you quantity as well quality. One prolific male porn star reputedly consumes two heads of celery the night before filming – for a 'shoot' to remember!

Biological benefits

The Aztecs were first in line to celebrate chocolate, holding riotous orgies to honor the harvest of the cacao bean. Chocolate contains PEA, or phenylethylamine, which is the same chemical that gives us the euphoric feeling we experience when we're newly in love. It's also full of antioxidants (the enzymes that help prevent cancer) and a caffeine-related substance called theobromine. For maximum benefit, the general rule of thumb is the darker the better, with at least 70% cocoa solids.

According to an Italian study, women who eat chocolate regularly have higher levels of desire and gain more satisfaction from sex. (As if we need an excuse.)

“There are a number of mechanical devices which increase sexual arousal, particularly in women. Chief among these is the Mercedes-Benz 380SL Convertible.”

P. J. O’Rourke

Ten top turn-ons to improve diminished desires

1. **Oysters** – highly nutritious, low in fat and loaded with zinc, which escalates production of sperm and testosterone. One of the classics.

2. **Cucumber** – Dr. Alan Hirsch, director of the Smell and Taste Research Foundation in Chicago, has discovered that women are hugely aroused by the smell of cucumber (not to mention being quite partial to their design…)

3. **Banana bread** – another stimulating aroma from Dr. Hirsch's findings. Also well designed, bananas are rich in potassium and energizing B vitamins, but it may be the "comforting and nostalgic smell" of banana bread that helps "women feel more relaxed". (And extremely hungry.)

4. **Cinnamon** – emerged as the favorite male whiff in Dr. H's scientific study of over 200 smells. Inhaling it gets blood racing to the penis, and cinnamon buns are particularly popular. Get baking girls…

5. **Watermelon** – mimics the effect of Viagra because of its citrulline content. Citrulline triggers the production of arginine, which in turn relaxes blood vessels – like the little blue pill. It's also an excellent source of lycopene, which can help prevent prostate cancer. You need to consume large amounts, but it's the perfect reason to get fruity.

6. **It's the pits** – the pheromonal oomph of a clean, freshly exercised armpit…sniff and sigh happy.

7. **Damiana** – a centuries-old South American aphrodisiac that can be taken as a supplement or drunk as a tea. Damiana contains gonzalitosin, which creates a feeling of gentle elation and a pleasant throbbing in his loins. Is that Damiana in your pocket – or are you just pleased to see me?

8. **Almonds** – a perennial symbol of fertility, almonds – like chocolate – are blessed with bags of phenylethylamine, the feel-good amino acid. They're also a first-rate source of essential fatty acids (good for male hormone production) and their smell is said to provoke passion in the fairer sex. Double marzipan on the Christmas cake, then.

9. **Liquorice** – the strong, serious, black kind. Chewing the root gives rise to lustful urges and makes women particularly wanton. You'll never look at Allsorts in the same way again.

10. **Putting the accent on sex** – OK, you might feel like a wally at first, but if she melts when you talk like George Clooney, or he can't get enough of your deep-throated drawl, where's the harm in humoring your loved one? A sexy voice resonates in more ways than one. After all, how many babies have been conceived with backing vocals provided by Barry White? I rest my case.

Fertility rights?

Recent studies into the possible links between baby gender and food intake at the time of conception, have concluded that a higher calorie intake can swing the odds in favor of boy babies. (In other words the more a woman eats, the more likely she is to have a son.)

The research offers an explanation for the decline of boy babies in the west, suggesting it's because we are now more prone to skipping breakfast and eating low fat foods. So, women wanting sons should have big bowls of cereal for brekky (with the occasional fry-up) and increase their daily intake by 400 calories. Big momma.

Chapter 14

Etiquette and Playing Safe

The idea of safer sex is nothing new, but its importance should never be underestimated. If you have unprotected sex with someone, you're effectively also having it with all the previous partners they've had unprotected sex with – so using the 'family tree' principle, you're sharing body fluids – and risks – with countless others. Scary.

To quote Suzi Godson, from her comprehensive The Sex Book, "The exchange of bodily fluids, however pleasant, has always been a dangerous occupation...teenagers sometimes believe that 'safe sex' simply means their parents won't catch them".

Misconceptions are still widely held, contributing to the significant increase of sexually transmitted infections (STIs) many of which have no visible symptoms. There's no way of knowing someone's sexual health from their outward appearance, so the only safe option is to take proper precautions – against diseases and pregnancy – and to discuss these precautions before you're overcome with desire. Although there's less danger of pregnancy post-50, we still need condoms as protection against a host of sexually transmitted infections. In less than a decade STIs have doubled in people over 45.

Safe sex overlaps into etiquette – the right thing is always to be safety conscious. If we're out there having sex with a new partner (or have several different relationships) we should all, men and women, carry condoms and never be shy about using them – it's crazy not to. Stay in control, minimize the risks, and take responsibility for your sexual health and well being.

A word of warning

If a vibrator or toy has an overpoweringly plastic smell when you open its box, don't use it without a condom. Phthalates are a class of chemical contaminants that are added to plastics to make them soft and pliable, and unfortunately many sex toys contain them (be especially cautious with any that are labelled "for novelty use only").

Laws were passed years ago restricting the type of plastics that could be used in baby toys – however there is currently limited legislation over sex toys, and phthalates have been linked to hormone disruption.

Rule of thumb – if it pongs, put a rubber on it.

Patience please

If there's something you like – a sexual activity or position – but your partner isn't good at it, be careful how you tell them. Make sure any criticism is always constructive so they can learn and improve. Harsh words that undermine and destroy confidence aren't going to win anybody any prizes. Insensitive comments about someone's technique will hurt and stay with them – and may put them off trying again!

The key to fulfilment for both of you is communication. Explain, teach and show each other what you enjoy, and give plenty of praise and encouragement along the way. It also helps to use "I" statements, as in "I love it when you do that" or "I don't feel good about that" – which show you're taking responsibility rather than putting pressure on your partner. Be honest – but be gentle and tactful.

Ow!

However generously endowed your man may be, never try bending his erect penis – believe it or not, it can break. It may be collapsible, but it's not designed to fold away...

“Some women say their best sex was not from those men who were the biggest or the longest; on the contrary it was with those men who were less well endowed, because they weren’t relying on only one body part to carry the show.”

Lou Paget

"Touching is a basic animal instinct… We crave the emotional nutrition that comes from touch, just like an essential vitamin… The truth is, we can't live without it. We develop a form of emotional scurvy, although we call it by different terms: depression, stress, anxiety, aggression, and midlife crisis… and treat it with drugs that don't work.

Lack of touch is just as detrimental to our health as a lack of vitamin C and just as easy to remedy."

Jean and Harvey Gochros

Wake-up call

If you keep promising your partner more sex, but you end up (understandably) so shattered from work/kids/life in general that you'd rather use your spare time to sleep, you may find yourself (understandably) a source of growing resentment.

Whether you're male or female, if your partner is important to you, don't ignore their needs. They've probably made it clear that they're disappointed when you don't keep your promises, so you need to schedule a proper 'sex date' in your diary (regardless of how contrived it feels, or how tired you are) and stick to it like any other arrangement. I'm not talking every night – but once a week, once a fortnight, or even once a month is great if there's been no nooky whatsoever.

It's easy to put sex on the back burner when you're tired and have so much else vying for your attention, but be careful – once you're out of the habit, your libido can suffer from the 'use it or lose it' syndrome. And don't always leave lovemaking until night time anyway – experiment with your body clock and maybe try setting your alarm twenty minutes earlier in the morning. You'll both reap the benefits...

Oops!

Odorless trapped air (nicknamed a 'queef') can sometimes escape from the vagina during, or after, intercourse. Rest assured that although it sounds horribly embarrassing, it is normal. You can minimize air intake by avoiding positions like doggie-style or with your legs in the air – plus your partner should avoid pulling right out and then thrusting deeply.

Twin-ply pleasure

On a practical note, kitchen roll is designed to be super absorbent – as we are reminded by endless TV commercials – but it doesn't have to be restricted to the kitchen. For post-coital clean-ups, a roll kept in the bedroom can be just as useful, and a lot more effective than flimsy tissues, which tend to break up. (Perhaps not the sort with pictures of chickens, though).

Sugar 'n' spice, not so nice

Don't insert any edibles into the vagina that might burn (like spicy foods), get stuck (marrow?!) or be difficult to retrieve (like grapes). Another no-no from the fruit bowl is a peeled banana, as it disintegrates easily and the high sugar content can lead to yeast infections like thrush. Your local greengrocer can supply far better substitute dildos (see Try this for size, page 115).

The same goes for any sweet foods that may interfere with the sensitive pH balance down below, including chocolate. Keep your choc-fix above waist level, as the oil in it can burn holes in latex condoms and chocolate can also leave embarrassing brown streaks on your sheets – could be slightly worrying for a new partner…

No-blow zone

It's fun to experiment, but be careful never to blow air into the vagina during oral sex – the outcome could be fatal. There is a danger it could create an air bubble, or embolus, that might obstruct the flow of blood through a vein or artery. Not worth the risk.

The sound of silence

If your partner is totally silent in bed, not even uttering the tiniest of sighs (believe me, I've been there) you need to explain to them how difficult it is for you to gauge their enjoyment. For all you know they could be in silent ecstasy or bored rigid.

Ask them to help you out with a few sighs, groans or words – even "yes" or "don't stop" is an indication that you're getting it right, and they're liking what you're doing. Lead by example with your own sexy whispers and sounds – and make sure you let them know what a turn-on it is for you when they reciprocate.

The condom, translated

Germany: Lummelute ("naughty bags")

Spain: Globo ("balloon")

Indonesia: Koteca ("penis gourd")

Portugal: Camisa de Venus ("Venus's shirt")

Greece: Kapota ("overcoat")

Hong Kong: Pei dang vi ("bulletproof vest")

Hungary: Osver ("safety tool")

Denmark: Gummimand ("rubber man")

France: La Capote Anglaise ("English raincoat")

Mexico: Angel custodio ("guardian angel")

China: Baoxian ("insurance glove")

Nigeria: Okpuamu ("penis hat")

Do's and don'ts for rubber goods

The best way to protect yourself is by using condoms. Actually, the best way to protect yourself is by using condoms correctly. They're inexpensive and available everywhere (in different sizes – including extra-large for those more generously endowed), so here are some useful do's & don'ts…

Do use a condom every time. They prevent unwanted pregnancy and protect against unwanted STIs and HIV – plus the range of all-singing, all-dancing, pleasure-enhancing varieties is extensive.

Do check the expiry date. Old condoms are more likely to split.

Do store them carefully, away from heat, wallets, pockets, and car glove compartments.

Do follow the instructions for putting on the condom; it's a process both sides can get involved in.

Don't wait until it's too late. If your bits are anywhere near your partner's bits, you should be wearing a condom.

Don't risk damaging a condom by using your teeth to open the packet.

Don't linger too long after the party's over – pull out as soon as you've come, with your penis still erect, whilst holding the rubber ring at the base.

Don't flush! Latex is a notorious drain clogger. Tie a knot in it, admire your virility – then bin it.

Warm up first

Before putting a condom on, pop a little drop of latex-friendly lube inside it. It'll heat everything up once you get going, so it mimics the warmth and wetness of the vagina and feels more like the real deal. Smear some on the outside for her pleasure too…

Four things not to have in your bedroom

1. **A television.** Studies have shown that couples with a TV in their bedroom make love half as often as those who keep it a screen-free zone. And the electromagnetic waves they emit (even in standby) don't make for sweet dreams either. Computers, mobiles and chargers are also a complete no-no (plus they remind you of work). Basically, no electrical devices in the bedroom – unless they're designed for your mutual pleasure...

2. **Photos of friends and family.** It's not easy to lose yourself in a thundering orgasm if your mum and dad are grinning at you from your bedside table. Much as you love them – and your angelic offspring – uninhibited sex will be more achievable if they're not watching, so make a home for them elsewhere.

3. **Mess.** Meaning all our junk and clutter which often ends up on the floor. And don't just shove it under the bed either – it makes for a high sneeze factor and causes stagnant energy to be trapped. In Feng Shui terms (the ancient oriental art of placement) this can lead to health problems and disturbed nights (but not in the way you'd want them to be). Manky knickers and soiled sheets may have worked brilliantly for Tracy Emin, but they're not generally top of the list for a good sex life, so freshen up now.

4. **Single images.** Another Feng Shui tip is to avoid pictures portraying a single person or image, as this may then be reflected in your relationships – or lack of them. Pictures depicting couples are a far more positive influence in a bedroom, promoting equality and harmony. So whether you're looking for a relationship or wanting to sustain one, surround yourself with pairs rather than singles.

“My girlfriend always laughs during sex – no matter what she’s reading.”

Steve Jobs, Founder, Apple Computers

Recommended reading...

Title	Author	ISBN
SEX by Numbers	Sarah Hedley	978-0-74992696-0
Superhotsex	Tracey Cox	978-0-75662275-6
Sex: How to do Everything	Em & Lo	978-1-40532896-8
The Sex Book	Suzi Godson with Mel Agace	978-1-84403511-3
Tickle His Pickle: Your Hands-On Guide to Penis Pleasing	Dr. Sadie Allison	978-0-97066112-8
Sex for One	Betty Dodson, Ph.D.	978-0-51788607-6
O: The Intimate History of the Orgasm	Jonathan Margolis	978-0-09944155-7
Incredible Sex	Marcelle Perks and Elisabeth Wilson	978-1-90490233-1
The Ex Factor	Emily Dubberley	978-1-90574517-3
269 Amazing Sex Tips and Tricks for Men	Anne Hooper and Phillip Hodson	978-1-86105958-1
She Comes First: The Thinking Man's Guide to Pleasuring a Woman	Ian Kerner, Ph.D.	978-0-28563722-1
Fabulous Foreplay	Dr. Pam Spurr	978-1-90621705-1
The Men's Health Guide to the Best Sex in the World	Rodale Press	978-1-59486726-2
The New Joy of Sex	Alex Comfort MB and Susan Quilliam	978-1-84533429-1

Title	Author	ISBN
The Book of Weird Sex	Chris Gordon	978-0-74908346-5
Improving your Relationship for Dummies	Paula Hall	978-0-47068472-6
7 Days to Amazing Sex	Sarah Hedley	978-0-74994090-4
Hot Sex: How to Do It	Tracey Cox	978-0-55214707-1
Too Young to Get Old	Christine Webber	978-0-74994276-2
Tricks to Please a Woman	Jay Wiseman	978-1-89015940-5
The Kama Sutra of Vatsyayana	Sir Richard Burton	978-0-48645237-1
"Ann Summers" Raunchy and Rampant Guide to Sex Toys	Ann Summers	978-0-09191643-5
How to Give Her Absolute Pleasure	Lou Paget	978-0-74992262-7
Put What Where?	John Naish	978-0-00721423-5
Dr. Ruth's Sex After 50	Dr. Ruth K. Westheimer	978-1-88495643-0
The Big Book of Filth	Jonathon Green	978-0-30435350-7
The Ultimate Guide to Anal Sex for Women	Tristan Taormino	978-1-57344221-3
Women's Pleasure	Rachel Swift	978-0-33033325-2
Female Ejaculation & the G-Spot	Deborah Sundahl	978-0-89793380-3
Cosmopolitan: Over 100 Triple X Sex Tricks	Lisa Sussman	978-1-84442480-1

Thanks to...

There are many people who have helped in the writing of this book and my collective thanks to you all (as some of you don't want to be individually named!)

My special thanks however to the following:

Harshad Kotecha and **Janet Hai** for their kindness, wisdom, encouragement and optimism; **Steve Brookes** for giving me the opportunity to write this book and **Tracy Staskevich** for her style and humor.

I am very grateful to **Sarah Hedley** for her kindness in writing the foreword, and to **Tracey Cox**, **Dr. Catherine Hood**, **Jenni Trent Hughes** and **Mimo Antonucci** for their endorsements. Thanks too to my inspirational agent and dear friend, **Julia Champion**, whose encouragement has been so valuable.

Huge thanks to my treasured family and friends, for their love and belief in me, which has meant so much. My daughter **Kate McEnery**, my sister **Lilian**, and my amazing brother **David** who was a real inspiration. Thanks too to **Peter Probert** and **Charlie**, **Bridget Brice (BB)**, **Sha**, **Heather**, **Lizzy Watson**, **Mike** and **Di Turner**, **David Charles** and **Mufrida Hayes**, **Victoria**, **Dom & Sharon**, **Jane**, **The GG's**, **Polly**, **Sue** & **Adrian**, **Franko**, **Kate Nicholls**, **Jane Cotton**, **NRJ**, **Jos** & **Steve**, **Clarissa** and **Robin**, **Evan**, **Jackie Llewelyn-Bowen**, **Mikhail**, **Mary Danson-Hill** and **Jess Greatrex**.

And I'm particularly grateful to **Wendy Turner-Webster**, **Penny** and **Vince**, **Lindsay Henson**, **Jan Holt**, **Trevor McCallum**, **Da'aboth Te'he'Ling**, **Maggie Kruger** and **Kevin Dunn**, for their extra-special support.

Thanks to **Megan Louise Roberts** for her shining enthusiasm and generosity of spirit; **Ruth Wilkinson** for her knowledge, dedication and advice; **Laura Tindorf, Katie Byrne, Sophie Barton** and the team at **Ann Summers** for being so welcoming and helpful, and giant thanks to **Richard Longhurst, Neal Slateford** and **Bonny Hall** at the fantastic www.LoveHoney.co.uk for their help, generosity, sheer creative genius and astounding delivery speeds! Big thanks too to **Richie** and **Jane Bowles** at www.idlube.co.uk and www.monogamyonline.com for all their amazing support.

Thanks also to the following for their generosity:
The ever stylish **Vanessa Munnings** and all at www.durex.com
Amy P. Sung, Brian Mayfield, and the team at www.aneros.com
Teri Baker at www.minikinicolour.com
Dr. Pam Spurr, Emily Dubberley, Suzi Godson, Mark Maffia, Pauline Morrison, Val Sampson, Em & Lo, Gary Starkie, Dr. Yvonne K. Fulbright, Jay Leno, Woody Allen, Toni Weschler, Dr. Sadie Allison, Anne Hooper, Chris Gordon, Dr. Ruth K. Westheimer, Betty Dodson, Lou Paget, Jean and **Harvey Gochros**, and **Steve Jobs**. www.starma.com (Muffy's world of vagina euphemisms) and www.sexlexis.com and the teams at www.FairyGothMother.co.uk and www.bondagetape.com

And last but never least, I am most grateful to my husband **Patrick Pearson**, for his brilliant editing skills, for his gentleness, and for always remaining calm. Thank you for being adventurous enough to test numerous toys with me; for putting up with me when I've been stressed and horrible; for cooking the best roast chicken in the world; and for making me laugh so much.

With love, Julie x

Index